ALL NEW 100 MATHS LESSONS

OMEWORK & ASSESSMENT

YEAR R

Ann Montague-Smith

Credits

Author
Ann Montague-Smith

Editor
Sally Gray

Assistant Editor
Aileen Lalor

Illustrations
Cathy Hughes and Baz Rowell

Series Designer
Catherine Mason

Designer
Catherine Mason

© 2006 Scholastic Ltd. Text © Ann Montague-Smith
Designed using Adobe InDesign

Published by Scholastic Ltd
Villiers House
Clarendon Avenue
Leamington Spa
Warwickshire CV32 5PR

www.scholastic.co.uk

Printed by Bell and Bain Ltd, Glasgow.

1 2 3 4 5 6 7 8 9   6 7 8 9 0 1 2 3 4 5

ACKNOWLEDGEMENTS

The publishers gratefully acknowledge permission
to reproduce the following copyright material:
Brenda Williams for the use of 'Ten Crafty
Crocodiles' and 'Ladybird Spots' by Brenda Williams
© 2005, Brenda Williams, previously unpublished

British Library Cataloguing-in-Publication Data
A catalogue record for this book is available from
the British Library.

ISBN 0-439-965-128
ISBN 978-0439-965125

The right of Ann Montague-Smith to be
identified as the author of this work has
been asserted by her in accordance with the
Copyright, Designs and Patents Act 1988.

Extracts from The National Numeracy Strategy
© Crown copyright. Reproduced under the terms
of HMSO Guidance
Note 8.

Due to the nature of the web, the publisher
cannot guarantee the content or links of any of
the websites referred to. It is the responsibility
of the reader to assess the suitability of
websites.

Every effort has been made to trace copyright
holders for the works reproduced in this book, and the
publishers apologise for any inadvertent omissions.

Contents

HOMEWORK

ASSESSMENT

Contents

ASSESSMENT

Introduction

About the series

All New 100 Maths Lessons; Homework and Assessment is a complete solution to your planning and resourcing for maths homework and assessment activities. There are seven books in the series, one for each year group from Reception to Year 6.

Each book contains approximately 57 homework activities, with activity sheets to take home, and assessments for each half-term, end of term and end of year.

The homework and assessment activities support planning based on the NNS's Medium-Term Plans and sample unit plans, but using the language of the learning objectives for that year as they appear in the NNS *Framework for Teaching Mathematics (DfEE, 1999)*.

About the homework activities

Each homework activity is presented as a photocopiable page, with supporting notes provided in a grid of teachers' notes at the beginning of each term. There is a unit reference in the grid, which references the homework activity to the relevant unit in the NNS Medium-Term Plan. This grid is the only place in the book where the objectives and further details about the homework are provided. It is left to your professional judgement exactly when homework is set and followed up. There are mostly two, and occasionally one, homework activities to support each NNS unit.

Maths to share

Across the series, the homework activities cover the range of homework types suggested by the National Numeracy Strategy. For Reception, these include 'Maths to share' activities and 'Puzzles to do at home'.

'Maths to share' activities encourage the children to discuss the homework task activity with a parent or carer, and may involve the home setting, or a game that can be played with the carer. These activities can be used to help children who would benefit from this further support at home, as well as providing ideas for parents and carers to extend the children's understanding through home activities. In this book, you will find number rhymes to learn, games to play, searches at home for patterns and shapes and so on. The activities use the home context wherever possible.

'Puzzles to do at home' are investigations or problem-solving tasks. Again, the parent or carer is encouraged to be involved with the activity, offering support to the child, and discussing the activity and its outcomes with the child.

Using the homework activities

Each homework page includes a 'Helper note' which explains, for an interested adult, the aim of the homework and how to support their child if he or she cannot get started. Some form of homework diary should be used alongside these activities, through which you can establish an effective dialogue about the children's enjoyment and understanding of the homework. A homework diary page is supplied on page 8 for your use.

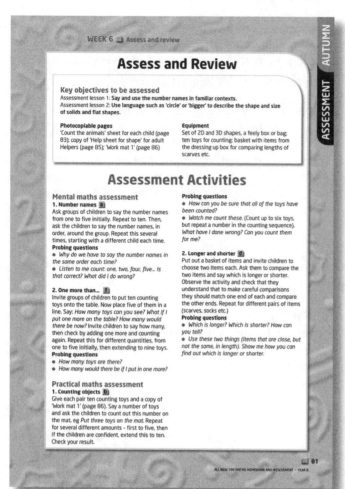

The teachers' notes for each term are set out in a grid format, and each termly grid sets out the following:

● The homework title.

● The NNS Learning objective/s (including the Key objectives) are covered by the homework activity (specific to the Medium-Term Plan). This will be useful as part of ongoing teacher assessment to show how well the children have understood the concepts being taught.

● The content of the homework – briefly describing the format and content of the activity to help the teacher to make a decision about which homework activity to choose.

● Managing the homework – in this section there are suggestions for explaining the homework to the children, such as telling the children why they will be doing this activity, or a brief oral activity to undertake as preparation for the homework. There are also suggestions about how to manage the review of the homework when the children return with it to school. Suggestions include discussing strategies used for solving a problem, comparing solutions and playing a game as a class.

● Links to *All New 100 Maths Lessons* – there are two references to the companion book *All New 100 Maths Lessons Reception* (Scholastic). There is a reference to the appropriate unit, with a page reference to the beginning of that unit. This will enable the teacher to compare what is being taught that week with the homework, so that the teacher can decide which homework to choose and when to send it home.

Developing a homework policy

The homework activities in this book have been written with the DfES 'Homework guidelines' in mind. These can be located in detail on the DfES Standards Site: **www.standards.dfes.gov.uk/homework/goodpractice/**

Encouraging home-school links

An effective working partnership between teachers and parents and carers can have a positive impact on children's attainment in maths. The homework activities in this book are part of that partnership. Parents and carers are given guidance on what the homework is about, and on how to be involved with the activity. There are suggestions for helping children who are struggling with a particular concept – for example, children who need extra help with counting can be encouraged in counting on or back and counting mentally by co-ordinating touching, moving and saying the number name. There are also extension ideas for children who would benefit from slightly more advanced work. These support and extension activities can be given out on a regular basis or used as specific support where children would benefit. At this level, homework may be less about academic attainment, and more about establishing a positive and supportive relationships between you and the parents and carers.

The homework diary page, sent home with the homework activity, with opportunities for children and parents to respond, can be found on page 8.

Using the assessment activities

For assessment, there are activities to support the assessment lessons built into the NNS Medium-Term Plan, for example, weeks 6 and 12 in the autumn term of Reception. The assessment tasks are built around the Key objectives taught during the preceding half-term and all objectives taught are covered in the appropriate assessment. See the Assessment introduction on page 82 for more guidance on how to use the assessment activities in this book.

Parent and teacher meetings

The assessment activities in this book can be used in parent or carer discussions with the teacher. The outcomes of the assessment activities, which cover the Key objectives taught in that half-term, term or year, will give good evidence for the teacher and parents/carers about how well the child is performing for the year group.

Using the activities with *All New 100 Maths Lessons Year R*

The activities, both homework and assessment, fit the planning within *All New 100 Maths Lessons.* As teachers plan their work on a week-by-week basis, so the homework activities can be chosen to fit the appropriate unit of work.

Homework diary

Name of activity & date sent home	Child's comments		Helper's comments	Teacher's comments
	Did you like this? Draw a face on the bear. 😊 😕 a lot a little not much	How much did you learn? Draw a face on the bear. 😊 😕 a lot a little not much		

PHOTOCOPIABLE

www.scholastic.co.uk

Activity name	Learning objectives	Content of homework	Managing the homework	All New 100 Maths Lessons Year R	
				NNS	Page
Number rhymes for 1 and 2	● **Say and use the number names in order in familiar contexts.**	Counting nursery rhymes for the numbers 1 and 2 for use at home.	**Before:** Say the rhymes to the children, with actions, several times so that the children begin to join in. **After:** Repeat the rhymes together, with actions, over time so that the children know the rhymes well.	1	8
Ten little monkeys	● **Say and use the number names in order in familiar contexts.**	A counting rhyme that extends the counting experience to 10.	**Before:** Say the rhyme to the children. Encourage them to hold up the correct number of fingers for each set of monkeys. **After:** Invite confident children to say the rhyme and ask the other children to hold up the correct number of fingers.	1	8
Counting rhymes up to five	● **Say and use the number names in order in familiar contexts.**	A counting rhyme for the numbers four and five. Involves counting the spots on a ladybird.	**Before:** Say the rhyme to the children, demonstrating the actions. Repeat this several times so that the children can join in. **After:** Encourage the children to say the rhyme with actions. Repeat this over time.	1	8
Counting at home	● **Count reliably up to 10 everyday objects.**	Provides examples of possible counting situations at home, such as four socks in a row.	**Before:** Explain that you would like the children to find things to count at home. Encourage them to give examples. **After:** Ask for examples of things that children found to count. Invite individuals to demonstrate how they counted, using sets of toys.	2	15
Shape search	● Use language such as circle or bigger to describe the shape and size of solids and flat shapes.	Involves finding shapes at home and describing them in order to encourage the children to use the language of shape.	**Before:** Show the children some 3D shapes and ask them to point to the pictures of these on the sheet. **After:** Ask the children to say some of the things that they found at home which were shaped like spheres, cubes...	3	21
Make a face	● Use a variety of shapes to make models, pictures and patterns and describe them.	Uses 2D shapes to make pictures.	**Before:** Explain the activity to the children. Discuss which shape might be used for the nose, eyes... **After:** Encourage the children to bring their finished sheets back to school. Discuss what they did. Make a display or book of the finished sheets.	3	21

NNS OBJECTIVES ▭ Teacher's notes

Activity name	Learning objectives	Content of homework	Managing the homework	All New 100 Maths Lessons Year R	
				NNS	Page
Counting cats	● **Count reliably up to 10 everyday objects.**	Provides picture cards for the children to count, encouraging them to co-ordinate touching and counting.	**Before:** Encourage the children to count by touching and saying the number. **After:** Using an A3 enlargement of the cards, ask ten children to hold them at the front of the class. Now invite the other children to order the children according to the card they hold.	4	28
Longer and shorter	● **Use language such as more or less, longer or shorter… to compare two quantities.**	Find objects that are longer and shorter than the picture on the sheet. Helps the child to recognise 'longer than' and 'shorter than' in everyday life.	**Before:** Use a ribbon. Ask the children to find things in the classroom longer/shorter than the ribbon. **After:** Invite the children to find things in the classroom longer than/shorter than/about the same length as the dog.	4	30
Ten in the bed	● Begin to recognise none and zero in stories, rhymes and when counting.	A counting rhyme that ends with zero to help children to recognise zero as 'nothing left'.	**Before:** Say the rhyme to the children several times so that they begin to join in. Ask them to hold up the relevant number of fingers for each verse. **After:** Say the rhyme together, over time, showing the relevant number of fingers for each verse.	5	36
Find one more than	● **Find one more… than a number from 1 to 10.**	A 'one more than' game for the children to play at home.	**Before:** Ask the children to hold up three fingers. Say: *How many is one more than three?* Ask the children to demonstrate by holding up another finger. **After:** Repeat the activity with the children. Ask: *How did you work this out?*	5	38
How many?	● **Say and use the number names in order in familiar contexts**, such as number rhymes, songs, stories, counting games and activities (first to 5, then 10, then 20 and beyond).	A Pelmanism game to play at home. Helps the child to recognise 'how many' and to say the number name in a game context.	**Before:** Make an A3 enlarged set of the dog cards. Ask twelve children to each hold up a card. Invite the others to say the names of children holding a matching pair of cards. **After:** Ask the children to use the cards, in pairs to play Snap.	7	43

NNS OBJECTIVES 🖵 Teacher's notes

Activity name	Learning objectives	Content of homework	Managing the homework	All New 100 Maths Lessons Year R	
				NNS	Page
More and fewer	● **Use language such as more or less, greater or smaller to compare two numbers** and say which is more or less, and say a number which lies between two given numbers.	A counting game to be played at home. Helps the child to count and to say which of two sets contains more and which contains fewer objects.	**Before:** Invite a child to hold up some of their fingers. Hold up some of yours, but more than the child. Ask: *Who is holding up more/fewer fingers?* Repeat this for different quantities of fingers. **After:** Invite two children to each take a small handful of counting toys and to count these out for the others to see. Ask: *Does Jo have more/fewer than Lisa? Do they have the same amount?* Repeat with other children and quantities.	7	43
Count 6	● **Count reliably up to 10 everyday objects.**	Involves counting up to six objects in various everyday contexts.	**Before:** Together count out six toys. Do this several times with different toys. **After:** Invite the children to hold up six fingers. Discuss the different ways that this could be done, eg 1 finger from one hand and 5 from the other, 2 and 4 and so on.	8	52
Card count	● **Find 1 more or 1 less than a number from 1 to 10.**	Find the card with 1 more than and 1 less than a quantity from 2 to 9.	**Before:** Using an A3 enlargement of the cards, ask ten children to each hold a card. Ask the other children to order the cards. Then ask: *Which card has one more than...?* **After:** Repeat the activity with ten children holding the enlarged card. Ask the child who answers correctly to change places with the child holding the answer card. Ask: *Who is holding the card that is 1 more/fewer than ...?*	8	52
Build a model	● Use language such as circle or bigger to describe the shape and size of solids and flat shapes.	The children use construction kits, boxes, tins and so on, in order to make a model. They describe the shapes of objects that they use.	**Before:** Discuss with the children what sort of materials they have at home that they could use to build models. **After:** Using a construction kit, ask a child to choose the first shape for the robot. Invite a child at a time to choose a shape to build the robot. Discuss the shapes, and their properties.	9	57
Pattern search	● Talk about, recognise and recreate simple patterns.	The children search for patterns at home, such as those on curtains or clothes. They describe the patterns that they find.	**Before:** Using some wallpaper pieces discuss the patterns that the children can see. **After:** Enlarge the sheet to A3. Invite the children to describe the patterns that they can see.	9	60

NNS OBJECTIVES — Teacher's notes

Activity name	Learning objectives	Content of homework	Managing the homework	All New 100 Maths Lessons Year R NNS	Page
Which is heavier?	● **Use language such as more or less... heavier or lighter... to compare two quantities**, then more than two, by making direct comparisons of... masses.	Involves comparing weight by picking up two different items to be found at home, such as a tin of baked beans and an apple.	**Before:** Put out some classroom objects. Pass two of them around the group for the children to 'feel' to say which is heavier and which is lighter. **After:** Put out three items. Invite the children to decide by holding how to order the items. Check with a balance.	10	65
Little Bo Peep	● Begin to understand and use vocabulary of time. ● Sequence familiar events.	Involves sequencing pictures of Little Bo Peep, to tell the story of the nursery rhyme.	**Before:** Ask the children to say what they have done so far today. Encourage them to sequence events. **After:** Using an A3 enlargement of the Little Bo Peep cards, invite the children to order the cards. Say the rhyme together once the cards are ordered, pointing to each card at the relevant time.	10	65
Sorting coins	● Begin to understand and use the vocabulary related to money. Sort coins, including the £1 and £2 coins, and use them in role play to pay and give change.	A sorting activity involving the naming of coins.	**Before:** Put out several 1p, 2p, 5p and 10p coins. Ask the children to take turns to find the coin that you say. **After:** Using the same coins ask the children to discuss what is special about each coin, eg its size, colour, design...	11	73
Play shops	● Use developing mathematical ideas and methods to solve practical problems.	Uses 1p coins in a shopping context.	**Before:** Put out ten 1p coins. Invite a child to count out the number of coins you say, such as: *Count out 6 pence.* Repeat for different amounts. **After:** Set up a penny shop. Invite children to 'spend' the amount that you say, and to hand over the correct number of penny coins.	11	73

Name

Date

Number rhymes for one

◼ Sing or say these traditional rhymes with the actions.

Hey diddle dumpling my son John

Hey diddle dumpling my son John,
(Rocking child in arms.)
Went to bed with his trousers on,
(Pretend to pull up trousers.)
One shoe off and one shoe on,
(Point to one shoe, then the other shoe.)
Hey diddle dumpling my son John.
(Rocking child in arms.)

Hickory dickory dock

Hickory dickory dock
(Arms moving like a pendulum to represent a 'ticking' noise.)
The mouse ran up the clock.
(Both arms up in the air.)
The clock struck one;
(Hold up one finger.)
The mouse ran down,
(Point down.)
Hickory dickory dock.
(Arms moving like a pendulum to represent a 'ticking' noise.)

see Dear Helper notes for
'Number rhyme for two' (page 14)

Name

Date

Number rhyme for two

◼ Sing or say this traditional rhyme with the actions.

Two little dicky birds sitting on a wall

Two little dicky birds sitting on a wall,
(Hold up two fingers.)
One named Peter and one named Paul.
(One finger, then the other finger.)
Fly away Peter, fly away Paul,
(Flying motion with one hand, then the other, down into lap.)
Come back Peter, come back Paul.
(Flying motion with one hand, then the other, back up again.)

Dear Helper
Learning these number rhymes and saying them while doing the actions will help your child to begin to remember the numbers one and two in order. Your child may also begin to recognise how many one and two are. Say the rhymes together, with the actions. The rhymes can be said at any time: walking to school, preparing dinner, at bedtime... Make it a fun time!

PHOTOCOPIABLE

www.scholastic.co.uk

Name	Date

Ten little monkeys

- Say the rhyme through, making suitable actions.

- Ask your child to join in with you.

- Repeat it several times, so that your child begins to remember the words.

One little monkey swinging in a tree.
Two little monkeys splashing in the sea.
Three little monkeys playing on a swing.
Four little monkeys dancing in a ring.
Five little monkeys drinking lemonade.
Six little monkeys digging with a spade.
Seven little monkeys chasing pussy cats.
Eight little monkeys wearing funny hats.
Nine little monkeys nodding little heads.
Ten little monkeys sleeping in their beds.

Anonymous, from *Early Years Poems and Rhymes* by Jill Bennett (Scholastic)

Dear Helper
This rhyme encourages your child to begin to say the numbers to ten in order. Say the rhyme together, and make up some actions. Ask your child to hold up the correct number of fingers for each number said. Encourage your child to say the rhyme to others and to 'teach' them some actions.

Name _____   Date _____

Counting rhyme up to five

   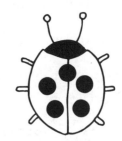

Ladybird spots

Catch a little ladybird
(Reach out, miming catching.)

Can you see?
(Point to palm of hand.)

One spot, two spots,
Another makes three.
(Count fingers.)

Catch another ladybird
(Reach out, miming catching.)

This has more.
(Point to palm of hand.)

One spot, two spots,
Three spots, four!
(Count fingers.)

Catch another ladybird
(Reach out, miming catching.)

Catch it live!
(Point to self.)

Count its spots
Right up to five!
(Hold up five fingers.)

One, two, three,
Four, five!
(Count fingers.)

Brenda Williams

Dear Helper
This rhyme encourages your child to count to five. Say the rhyme together and do the actions. Ask your child to show you how many one, two, three, four and five are using their fingers. Your child will enjoy teaching these rhymes, and the actions, to others.

PHOTOCOPIABLE

www.scholastic.co.uk

Counting at home

Dear Helper

Here are some suggestions for counting things together at home:

- Ask your child to put some objects in a line.
- Ask them to touch the first object, move it forwards and say the number name, doing these together.
- Now they move to the next object.
- This will help your child to know what they have counted and what is still to be counted.
- Ask your child to say how many there were.

Name

Date

Shape search

◗ Look at these pictures.

◗ Find some shapes at home like these.

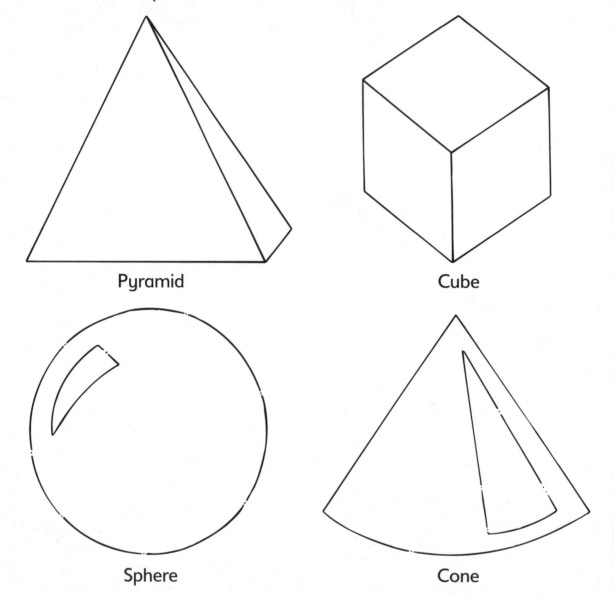

Pyramid

Cube

Sphere

Cone

Dear Helper

This activity helps your child to recognise 3D shapes and to begin to describe them. Encourage your child to look at each shape on the sheet in turn and to search for something similar in shape around the home. Ask questions such as: *What does this shape look like? Do you know what it is called?* The mathematical names of the shapes are beneath the pictures above.

Encourage your child to talk about the shape using language such as *flat, round, curved.* Your child will enjoy talking about everyday things with these shapes, such as balls, boxes, ice-cream cones, chocolate that comes in a pyramid shaped box, and so on.

PHOTOCOPIABLE

www.scholastic.co.uk

Make a face

- Cut out the shapes.
- Make a face with the shapes.

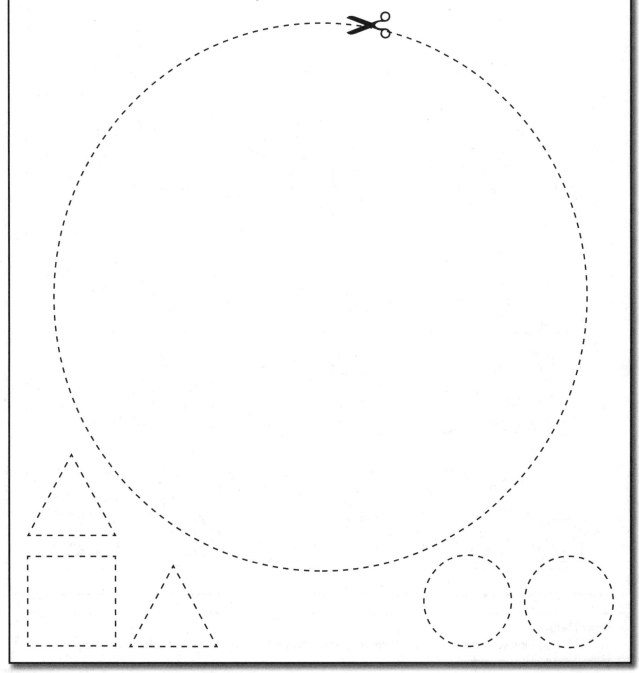

Dear Helper
This activity helps your child to begin to recognise 2D shapes and to name them. If your child finds cutting out difficult, do please help. Ask your child to decide what sort of face they would like to make. Talk about what each of the shapes represents, such as triangles for ears, or the small circles for eyes. Talk about the shape of the pieces, using language such as *round* or *straight*.

PHOTOCOPIABLE

www.scholastic.co.uk

Counting cats

■ Cut out the cards and count the cats.

Dear Helper

This activity helps your child to count objects. If your child finds cutting out difficult, please help them to cut out the cards

Begin with the cards with one, two and three cats on and ask your child to say how many are on each card. Encourage your child to look and say how many. From four cats on, ask your child to count the cats by touching each cat and saying the counting number. When your child has counted each cat, ask: *What was the last number you said? How many cats are there?*

When your child is confident with counting to ten, use bricks, or other toys, and encourage your child to count 11 or 12 of these.

Longer and shorter

- Cut out the dog.
- Find things longer than the dog.
- Find things shorter than the dog.

Dear Helper

This activity helps your child to recognise 'longer than' and 'shorter than'. If your child finds cutting out difficult, help them to cut out the dog.

Ask your child to look for things at home that are longer than the dog. Encourage him or her to make a direct comparison by placing the tail of the dog at one end of the thing being compared. Now ask your child to find things shorter than the dog picture. Ask your child: *How do you know that this is longer/shorter than the dog? Show me.*

When your child is confident with this activity, encourage them to choose three things and put them in order from shortest to longest.

PHOTOCOPIABLE

www.scholastic.co.uk

Name

Date

  # Ten in the bed

There were ten in the bed
And the little one said,
'Roll over, Roll over.'
So they all rolled over
And one fell out.

There were five in the bed
And the little one said,
'Roll over, Roll over.'
So they all rolled over
And one fell out.

There were nine in the bed
And the little one said,
'Roll over, Roll over.'
So they all rolled over
And one fell out.

There were four in the bed
And the little one said,
'Roll over, Roll over.'
So they all rolled over
And one fell out.

There were eight in the bed
And the little one said,
'Roll over, Roll over.'
So they all rolled over
And one fell out.

There were three in the bed
And the little one said,
'Roll over, Roll over.'
So they all rolled over
And one fell out.

There were seven in the bed
And the little one said,
'Roll over, Roll over.'
So they all rolled over
And one fell out.

There were two in the bed
And the little one said,
'Roll over, Roll over.'
So they all rolled over
And one fell out.

There were six in the bed
And the little one said,
'Roll over, Roll over.'
So they all rolled over
And one fell out.

There was one in the bed
And the little one said,
'Roll over, Roll over.'
So they all rolled over
And one fell out.

There were none in the bed.

Dear Helper
This rhyme helps your child to recognise that zero means 'nothing left'. Say it together, while looking at the pictures. Ask your child to count how many teddies are left each time. When you get to none, use the word zero. Ask your child to tell you what zero means.

www.scholastic.co.uk

Name	Date

Find one more than

◼ You will need ten pennies or counters.

Dear Helper

This activity helps your child to begin to recognise one more than a number between one and ten. Put the pennies onto the table. Ask your child to pick up three pennies. Ask them to count them out for you. Now say: *How many would there be if there was one more?* Ask your child to put one more and count to check. Repeat this for different amounts between one and nine, each time asking for one more. If your child finds this difficult, keep the amounts smaller – say, between one and three, four or five.

How many?

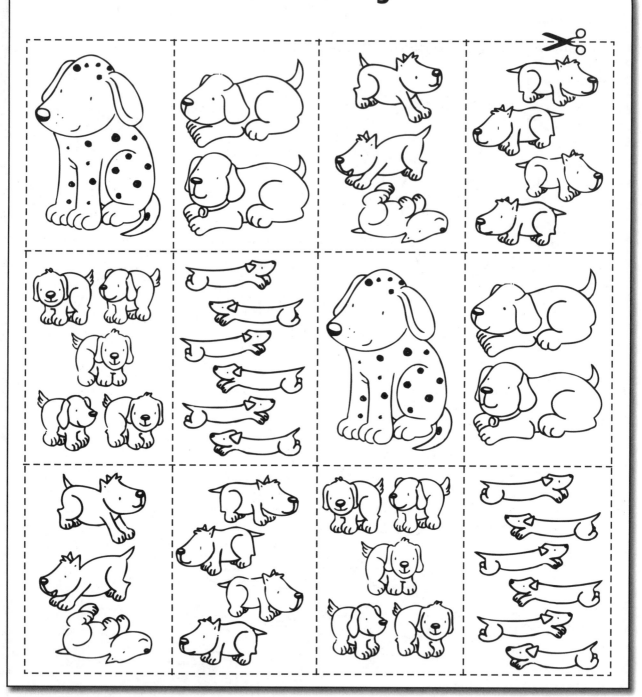

Dear Helper

This is a game called Pelmanism for you to play with your child. Cut the cards out and spread them out, face down. Take turns to choose two cards and turn them face up. If the cards match, take the cards; if they do not match, turn them face down again. The player with the most cards, when all the cards have been taken, is the winner.

Each time two cards are turned face up, ask your child to say how many dogs are on the card. If your child finds this game difficult, limit the cards to those with one, two and three dogs on. Then, over time, include four, five and then six dogs.

To challenge your child, this game can also be played with two sets of one to ten playing cards.

Name	Date

More and fewer

- You will need some large buttons, pennies or counters.

- Take turns to take a small handful of buttons.

- Count how many.

- Ask your child to say which handful has more and which has fewer.

Dear Helper

This activity helps your child to use the vocabulary of more and fewer when comparing the quantities in two sets. Encourage your child to begin with a small handful of buttons, up to about five. If your child takes too many, then consider using bricks or small toys instead in order to limit how many are taken each time.

Ask your child to count how many they have taken by putting the buttons on the table, in a row, and counting each one by touching and saying the counting number. They can then count how many you have in your handful. Ask: *Who has more? You or me? So who has fewer?* Repeat this several times.

Challenge your child to compare for more and fewer for amounts up to about ten.

Count six

◼ Find six of each of these things at home.

Dear Helper

This activity helps your child to count out six objects. If any of the things suggested are not readily available then use other things, such as tin cans or sweets.

Ask your child to find six forks. Ask them to put them in a line and to count each one by touching it and saying the number. When all have been counted, say: *What was the last number you said? How many forks are there?*

Repeat this for the other things to be counted. If your child finds this difficult, suggest that they begin by counting out a smaller number, such as three, four and five things.

Challenge your child to find seven, eight, nine or ten things and to count those.

PHOTOCOPIABLE

Card count

◢ Cut out the cards.

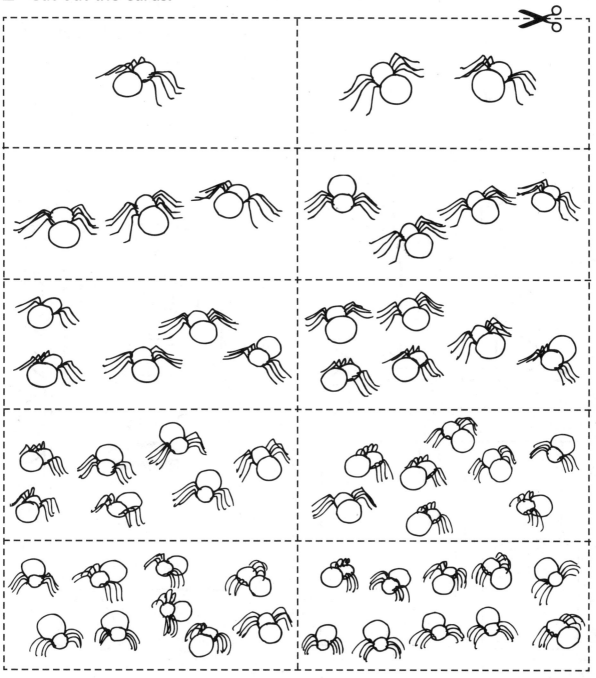

Dear Helper

This activity helps your child to count how many are on each card, and to find the card with one more or one fewer. Help your child to cut out the cards, then place them in a line on the table, but not in number order. Ask your child to choose a card, such as four. Say: *Find the card with one more than four.* If your child finds this difficult, count from one to four and say: *What comes after four?* When your child is confident with the idea of one more, say: *Find the card with one fewer than four.*

Name

Date

Build a model

◼ Use a construction kit, boxes or tins.

◼ Make a model with them.

◼ Talk about the model that you have made.

Dear Helper
This activity helps your child to use a construction kit, building blocks or boxes to make a model. Talk about which shapes are good for building and why. Encourage your child to describe the shape of the blocks that they are using. If your child is not sure about the shape names, offer words such as sphere (for a ball shape), cube, cone and pyramid. Challenge your child to make a model that uses a variety of shapes.

PHOTOCOPIABLE

Pattern search

- Look around you at home.

- Find some patterns.

- Talk about them.

Dear Helper

This activity helps your child to recognise and talk about patterns. Ask your child to walk around the house with you and to search for patterns. At first you may need to point out, for example, that a jumper has a patterned border. Discuss the pattern together. Look for the pattern repeating itself.

Challenge your child to find something patterned in each room in the house.

Name

Date

Which is heavier?

- Find some things at home that you can pick up.

- Choose two of them.

- Pick up one.

- Now pick up the other.

Dear Helper

This activity helps your child to find which is heavier and which is lighter by estimating. Encourage your child to find things that have clear differences in weight to begin with. When they are confident with this, extend to three objects and ask your child to order them from lightest to heaviest.

PHOTOCOPIABLE

www.scholastic.co.uk

Little Bo Peep

Little Bo Peep has lost her sheep
And doesn't know where to find them.
Leave them alone and they'll come home,
Wagging their tails behind them.

- Cut out the pictures.

- Put the pictures in order to tell the story.

Dear Helper

This activity encourages your child to sequence events. Read the nursery rhyme of 'Little Bo Peep' to your child two or three times, so that they begin to join in with you, if they do not already know it. Now ask your child to cut out the pictures. If they find this difficult, do help them! Ask your child to decide which picture comes first, and to explain why. Repeat this for all the pictures so that they are in order. Now ask your child to tell you the story of what is happening. Say the nursery rhyme together, pointing at each picture.

Sorting coins

◖ You will need several 1p, 2p, 5p and 10p coins.

◖ Put out the coins.

◖ Sort the coins so that all the 1p coins are together.

◖ Repeat this for the other coins.

| 1p | 2p | 5p | 10p |

Coins © The Royal Mint

Dear Helper

This activity helps your child to recognise and name coins. Ask your child to find all the 1p coins. If your child finds it hard to sort out the 1p coins, talk together about the size and colour of a 1p coin. Look together at a 1p coin. Ask your child to describe the pictures on the heads and tails sides of the coin, and to describe its colour. Now ask them to find all the 2p coins, and repeat this. Do this again for 5p and 10p coins.

Challenge your child to sort out and name 20p, 50p, £1 and £2 coins.

Play shops

- You will need ten 1p coins and some things for the shop.

- Everything in the shop costs 1p.

- Buy some things for 1p.

- Count out enough penny coins to pay for the shopping.

Dear Helper

This activity helps your child to pay for items using 1p coins. Choose some things for the shop. These could be tins of food, toys, or books. Alternatively, choose items from the picture on this sheet to buy.

You act as shopkeeper. Tell your child how much something is. At first, keep the price to 1p, then, over time, extend this to up to 5p, then 10p. When your child chooses something to buy, encourage them to count out the correct number of coins into your hand.

Challenge your child by asking them to be shopkeeper as you buy something and pay for it.

NNS OBJECTIVES 🗋 Teacher's notes

Activity name	Learning objectives	Content of homework	Managing the homework	All New 100 Maths Lessons Year 2	
				NNS	Page
One, two buckle my shoe	● **Say and use number names in order in familiar contexts**, such as number rhymes, songs, stories, counting games and activities (first to 5, then 10, then 20 and beyond).	A counting nursery rhyme to be recited with actions at home.	**Before:** Begin by saying the rhyme to just *Nine, ten...* Teach the children the actions. Extend to *Nineteen, twenty...* **After:** Say the rhyme together several times with the actions. Use the rhyme again, over time, as part of saying counting numbers in order.	1	82
Smaller and larger	● Order a given set of numbers, for example, the set of numbers 1 to 6 given in random order.	Activity involves ordering two quantities of items found at home.	**Before:** Invite a child to put a few counters out. Now ask another child to do this with and different quantity of counters. Ask: *Which set has more/fewer? How do you know?* **After:** Repeat the activity with all the children. Introduce a third quantity of counters and ask the children to order them from least to most; then most to least. Repeat this several times.	1	82
Combining	● **Begin to relate addition to combining two groups of objects.**	Activity involves combining two groups to find totals up to 10.	**Before:** Invite a child to count out two toys and to put them onto the table. Now ask another child to count out three toys and put these, separately onto the table. Ask: *How many are there altogether?* At this stage the children will probably count each set, then count all. **After:** Repeat the activity. Encourage the children to extend to larger quantities to a total of 6, 7, 8, 9 then 10.	2	91
Partitioning	● Separate (partition) a given number of objects into two groups.	Partitioning a group in different ways to find totals for 7.	**Before:** Invite the children to hold up seven fingers. Discuss the different ways in which they can do this: 2 and 5, 3 and 4, 4 and 3 and 5 and 2. **After:** Repeat the activity on the sheet with the children, this time for a total of 8.	2	92
Shape draw	● Begin to name solids such as a cube, cone, sphere... and flat shapes such as circle, triangle, square, rectangle...	Children are asked to find things at home to draw around to make outlines of circles, triangles, squares.	**Before:** Invite the children to take turns to choose from some shape tiles and to name and describe the 2D shapes. **After:** Invite the children to show their drawings. Ask them to name the shapes and what they used to make their drawings. Make a display of the completed sheets or put them into a book.	3	96

Activity name	Learning objectives	Content of homework	Managing the homework	All New 100 Maths Lessons Year 2	
				NNS	Page
Sorting	● Sort and match objects, pictures or children themselves, justifying the decisions made.	Children help at home to sort items of washing, when putting them away, describing why items belong in the same set.	**Before:** Put out some toys and ask children to make pairs. Ask them to explain why the two toys go together (size, colour, same toy...) **After:** Invite the children to help you to sort some items from the class shop. Ask: *Why do those belong together? What else could go into that set?*	3	100
One more, one fewer	● Recite the number names in order, continuing the count backwards or forwards from a given number.	Children count how many on a card, then say the number, then find the card which goes one before and one after that quantity.	**Before:** Explain the activity to the children using an A3 enlargement of the sheet. Choose a starting quantity of less than 5 cars. **After:** Use the enlarged cards to repeat the activity. This time invite a child to choose the start card, another to find the one fewer and another to find the one more. Discuss why a start card of one is not possible.	4	103
Water fun	● **Use language such as more or less,** to compare two quantities, then more than two, by filling and emptying containers.	Children fill and pour water from containers. In discussion they use the language of estimation and capacity.	**Before:** Demonstrate and discuss how to compare capacities by filling and pouring. **After:** Invite the children to choose two containers from a selection, estimate which holds more/less, then check by filling and pouring. Extend to ordering three capacities.	4	104
Take away	● **Begin to relate subtraction to taking away** and counting how many are left.	A subtraction game in which the child counts objects and makes subtraction sentences.	**Before:** Ask the children to hold up five fingers. Say: *Put down two. How many are left? So 5 take away 2 leaves 3.* Repeat for other subtraction sentences for 5. **After:** Invite a child to take a handful of counters and count them. Ask another child to say how many to take away. Now invite the children to say the subtraction sentence. Repeat for different starting quantities, up to 10.	5	110
Shopping	● Begin to understand and use vocabulary related to money. Sort coins, including £1 and £2 coins, and use them in role play to pay and give change.	A shopping game in which child 'buys' items for pennies.	**Before:** Invite a child to choose something from the shop such as a comic for 3p. Invite another child to count out the money in pennies. Repeat for other items. **After:** Explain that when someone buys something from the shop each time, for up to 5p, you want to know how many pennies are left from the 5 pennies each time.	5	113

NNS OBJECTIVES 🔲 Teacher's notes

Activity name	Learning objectives	Content of homework	Managing the homework	All New 100 Maths Lessons Year R	
				NNS	Page
Rhymes for 10	● **Say and use the number names in order in familiar contexts.**	Some counting rhymes designed to help children become more confident with counting to 10.	**Before:** Say the rhymes, holding up your fingers each time to show how many. Repeat several times so that the children begin to join in. **After:** Repeat the rhymes together, with counting finger actions. Repeat over time.	7	117
Numbers at home	● Recognise numerals 1 to 9.	Encourages children to find and read numerals at home, e.g. on books, cans, TV etc	**Before:** Discuss where children will find numbers at home: clock face, food packaging... **After:** Invite the children to say where they found numbers and what these numbers were. Write the numbers onto the flipchart.	7	117
Dotty numbers	● **Recognise numerals 1 to 9**, then 0 to 10, and beyond 10.	A dot-to-dot activity designed to practise putting numbers in order.	**Before:** Explain that the numbers on the sheet must be joined in number order in order to make the pictures. **After:** Using an A3 version of the sheet invite children to complete each picture. Ask: *What is the last number to make the ___?*	7	117
Animal add	● **Begin to relate addition to combining two groups of objects**, counting all the objects.	Counting two sets of pictures and saying how many there are altogether.	**Before:** Using an A3 enlargement of the sheet explain that each small picture shows adult and baby animals. **After:** Pin up the A3 enlargement of the sheet. Ask: *Which picture has 3 animals altogether? Say the addition sentence: 2+1=3.* Repeat for the other pictures.	8	124
Pattern search	● **Talk about, recognise and recreate simple patterns**, for example, simple repeating or symmetrical patterns in the environment.	Encourages children to find things at home that are patterned such as striped socks or patterned tiles. They then have to describe each pattern.	**Before:** Discuss where children might look for patterns at home. **After:** Ask the children to say what patterns they found and to describe them.	9	131
Where does it go?	● **Use everyday words to describe position**: for example, follow and give instructions about positions, directions and movements in PE and other activities.	The children are asked to position items on an outline picture.	**Before:** Using an A3 enlargement of the sheet invite the children to suggest where the items might go in the room. Ask them to bring their completed sheets back to school. **After:** Invite the children to show their completed sheets and to discuss where they placed the items. Check that they can use the relevant mathematical vocabulary. The sheets can be displayed or placed into a book.	9	131

NNS OBJECTIVES 🗋 Teacher's notes

Activity name	Learning objectives	Content of homework	Managing the homework	All New 100 Maths Lessons Year R	
				NNS	**Page**
Reading numbers	● **Recognise numerals 1 to 9**, then 0 to 10, then beyond 10.	A number card activity, in which children name the cards, and place them in order, from 1 to 9 or 0 to 10.	**Before:** Give further opportunities for reading numerals before the children take the sheet home. **After:** Invite each child to spread out the numerals 1 to 10. Explain that you will say a number. Ask them to hold up the relevant card when you say: *Show me*.	10	136
Make 10	● **Count reliably up to 10 everyday objects** (first to 5, then 10, then beyond), giving just one number name to each object.	A game designed to encourage accurate counting. The first player to collect 10 counters wins.	**Before:** Play a game: invite children to take turns to take a handful of counters, without counting. Those who then count to find they have ten win a point. **After:** Suggest that the children play the game in groups of four of five. Repeat this over time using different counting materials in order to improve estimation skills with differently sized objects.	11	145
Sorting	● Sort and match objects, pictures or children themselves, justifying the decisions made.	A sorting game, involving the use of picture tiles.	**Before:** Put out a selection of items from the room. Invite a child to sort the objects. Discuss how they have been sorted. Repeat for other sortings by different children, such as by colour, shape... **After:** Using an A3 enlargement of the sheet, ask: *How can we sort these?* Discuss the children's suggestions. If you have multiple copies of the sheet, then make the different sets that the children suggest and label them with the sorting.	11	145

Name   Date

One, two buckle my shoe

◼ Say the rhyme together and do the actions.

One, two, buckle my shoe
One, two, buckle my shoe.
(Do up shoe.)
Three, four, knock at the door.
(Knock with knuckles on the floor.)
Five, six, pick up sticks.
(Pretend to pick up sticks from the floor.)
Seven, eight, lay them straight.
(Mime putting sticks into a straight line.)
Nine, ten, a big fat hen.
(Making a large circle shape.)
Eleven, twelve, dig and delve.
(Child digging.)
Thirteen, fourteen, maids a-courting.
(Hold hands with next-door child.)
Fifteen, sixteen, maids in the kitchen.
(Pretend to cook.)
Seventeen, eighteen, maids in waiting.
(Stand with hands behind your back.)
Nineteen, twenty, my plate's empty.
(Rub tummy.)

Dear Helper
This activity helps your child to begin to learn the number names in order up to 20. Say the rhyme through together, and do the actions. Repeat this over time so that your child becomes familiar with the words and actions.
  When your child knows the rhyme well, encourage them to teach it to someone else. Challenge your child to say the counting numbers from one to 20.

www.scholastic.co.uk

Smaller and larger

- You will need: two pots and ten coins.

- Put some coins into one pot and some into the other.

- Make sure that the amounts in each pot are different.

- Count how many coins are in each pot.

- Decide which has more and which has fewer.

Dear Helper

This activity helps your child to recognise which is a larger and which a smaller amount. If your child finds counting difficult, begin by limiting the count to no more than three or four in each pot. Ask: *Which pot has more coins? Which has fewer coins?*

When your child is confident with this, introduce a third pot, and some more coins. Repeat the activity, and this time ask your child to put the pots in order, from least to most coins.

Name   Date

Combining

- You will need: ten counters or coins and a paper bag.

- Put the counters into the bag.

- Now put some of the counters onto the dog and some onto the cat.

- Count the counters on the dog and cat.

- Count all of the counters.

- Put the counters onto the animals three more times in different ways.

Dear Helper

This activity helps your child to begin to see that combining two groups is adding. When your child has put the counters on the cat and dog, say: *Count the dog counters. Count the cat counters. Now count all of the counters.*

Now talk about adding. For example, for five counters on the dog and one on the cat, say together: *five add one is six.* Challenge your child to try this activity with more than ten counters.

PHOTOCOPIABLE

www.scholastic.co.uk

Name   Date

Partitioning

- You will need seven counters.

- Put some of the counters onto the frog.

- Put the other counters onto the fish.

- Count how many are on the frog.

- Count how many are on the fish.

- Count all of the counters.

- Do this three more times in different ways.

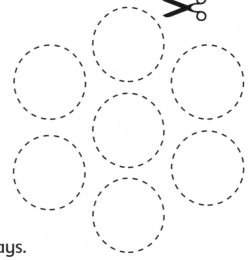

Dear Helper

This activity helps your child to separate a quantity into two sets and to find that the total is still the same. When your child has moved counters to the frog and to the fish, say: *Count the counters on the frog. Count the counters on the fish. Now let's count all of the counters.* For example, for four and three say *four add three is seven.*

Challenge your child to repeat this activity, this time for eight counters.

Name   Date

Shape draw

- Find some things at home to draw round.

- Find things to make a circle, a triangle and a square.

- Draw them here.

Dear Helper

This activity helps your child to recognise that solid shapes can have faces that are circular, square or triangular. Ask your child to try different things at home, and to sort them by the shape made when they draw around them on paper. If your child finds it hard to recognise what will be drawn, ask them to trace a finger around the edge of the object and to describe what they feel – whether it is curved, or has straight lines.

 Challenge your child to find things that have both curved and straight edges and then to draw around those.

PHOTOCOPIABLE

www.scholastic.co.uk

Name   Date

Sorting 1

- Help to sort the washing.

- Put things that are the same in one pile.

Dear Helper

This activity helps your child to sort for a given criterion. Ask your child to sort some real washing with you. As you do this, talk about which items belong in which pile, and why. For example: *This is James' washing... All the socks go in this pile.* When sorting into pairs, encourage your child to explain why particular socks make a pair.

   Ask your child to suggest other things that can be sorted at home, such as cutlery when washing-up or different types of food when you have been shopping.

One more, one fewer

- Cut out the cards.

- Choose a card.

- Count how many cars are on it.

- Find the card that is one fewer.

- Find the card that is one more.

- Say the three numbers in order.

- Do this again four times.

Dear Helper

This activity helps your child to say the number that is one more, and one less than a given number, from one to ten. Begin with a small quantity, such as the card with three on it.

If your child finds this activity hard, help them to count from one to three, and to say which is the number before three, then to count beyond three, to four.

Challenge your child to say the number that is one more or one less than any number from one to ten. Extend this to numbers to 15, then to 20 over time.

PHOTOCOPIABLE

Name	Date

Water fun

- You will need some plastic containers that are safe to use in the bathroom.

- This activity would be good as part of bathtime.

- Choose two containers.

- Decide which holds more and which holds less.

- Check by pouring and filling.

- Do this again for other containers.

Dear Helper

This activity helps your child to use the vocabulary of estimation and of capacity. Ask questions such as: *Which do you think holds more/less? Why do you think that? How can you check?*

When your child has compared three or four containers, ask them to choose one of them. Give some instructions such as: *Fill it up! Pour out the water so that it is nearly empty. Now make it half-full... nearly full...* Have some fun!

45

Name   Date

Take away

- You will need: ten counters or pennies and two plates.

- Take a small handful of counters and put them onto a plate.

- Count them.

- Now ask your Helper to take some of these counters and put them onto the other plate and count them.

- Say a subtraction sentence.

- Do this again four times

Dear Helper
This activity helps your child to begin to use the vocabulary of subtraction. For example, if your child puts five counters onto the plate, you might take three and put them onto the other plate. Say: *How many counters have I taken?* Ask your child to count the counters, touching each one. Now say together: *So five take away three leaves two.* If your child finds this activity difficult, count the counters together, out loud.

Challenge your child to try some subtractions, starting with nine or ten counters.

Name   Date

Shopping

◢ You will need: ten pennies and some things to buy.

◢ Choose something to buy.

◢ Ask your Helper how much it is.

◢ Count out the pennies to pay for it.

Dear Helper
This activity helps your child to begin to understand and use the vocabulary of money. Begin with lower prices, from 1p to 5p. Ask your child to count out the correct number of penny coins each time.
   If your child finds this difficult, count the coins together, with your child touching and moving the coins until they have counted out enough.
   Challenge your child by asking them to say how much they have left from the ten 1p coins each time.

Name   Date

Rhymes for ten

- Say the rhymes together.

- Repeat them several times so that your child begins to know the words.

- Hold up fingers to show how many each time.

Ten tall soldiers
Ten tall soldiers
Standing in a row,
Five stood up
And five lay low.
Along came the sergeant
And what do you think?
Up popped the other five
Quick as a wink.

Ten galloping horses
Ten galloping horses came into town,
Five of them were white and five were brown.
First they galloped up, then they galloped down;
Ten galloping horses came into town.

Dear Helper
Reciting these rhymes will help your child with the numbers to ten. Your child has begun to learn these rhymes at school. Say the rhymes together several times so that your child begins to know the words. Ask your child to show you each number, as it comes in the rhyme, with that quantity of fingers.

When your child can confidently say one of the rhymes, suggest to them that they teach it to someone else.

PHOTOCOPIABLE

Name	Date

Numbers at home

- ◀ Find numbers at home.

- ◀ Find as many as you can.

- ◀ Read them with your Helper.

Dear Helper

This activity helps your child to recognise numerals. Begin with numerals one to five, and search together for places where these might be found, such as on food packets or in books.

When your child is confident with these, extend the range to nine.

Challenge your child to find numerals for ten and beyond.

Name   Date

Dotty numbers

■ Join the numbers in order.

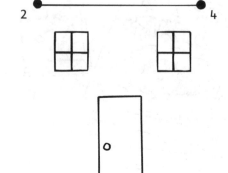
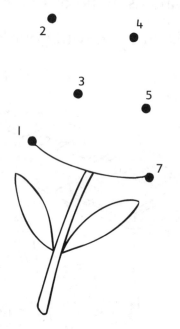
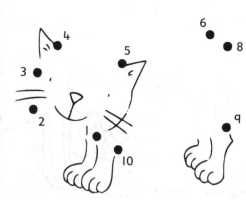
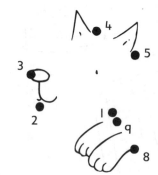

Dear Helper

This activity helps your child to read numbers. Talk about the numbers that your child can see in the picture, and encourage them to say the numbers in order. If your child finds this difficult, say the counting numbers together, and write these down for them in order. Your child may like to colour in the pictures once the dots have been joined.

Challenge your child to say the final number for each picture and to say the number that is one more and one less.

Name _____   Date _____

Animal add

- ◀ Count the first set of animals.

- ◀ Count the second set of animals.

- ◀ Count all the animals.

- ◀ Say an addition sentence.

Dear Helper

This activity helps your child to add by counting all. Begin by talking about the first picture. Ask: *How many kittens are there? And how many cats? Let's count them all to find how many altogether?* Then say an addition sentence together: *two add one is three.* Repeat this for the other animal sets.

Challenge your child to draw their own sets of animals and to say addition sentences for these.

Name ....   Date ....

Say the pattern

- ◾ Find something at home which has a pattern.

- ◾ There are some ideas in the pictures below.

- ◾ Find three more things with patterns to describe.

Dear Helper

This activity helps your child to recognise and describe patterns. Ask your child to 'say' the pattern, for example: *train, car, train, car...* . If they find this difficult, do this together. Now ask your child to 'say' the pattern themselves. Ask: *What would come next in the pattern? And next?*

Challenge your child to find more complicated patterns and to 'say' these, too.

PHOTOCOPIABLE

www.scholastic.co.uk

Name	Date

Where does it go?

- You will need: scissors and glue.

- Cut out the pictures below.

- Ask your Helper to tell you where to put the pictures.

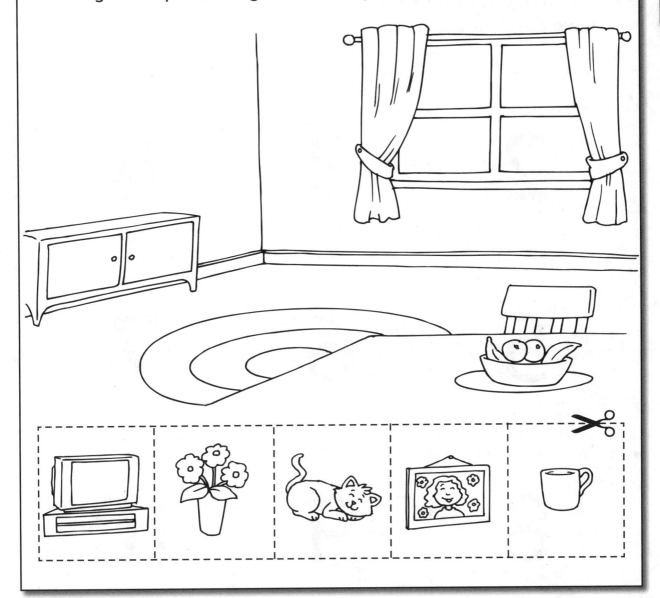

Dear Helper

This activity helps your child to understand and to use position words. Say, for example: *Put the cat on the rug; put the vase on top of the table; put the television by the chair on the floor; put the mug beside the chair.*

   Check that your child places the pictures correctly, then suggest that they move some of them to new positions, encouraging your child to say where the picture is, using position words.

   Challenge your child by asking questions about the position of things in your own home so that your child describes where they are.

Reading numbers

- Cut out the cards and shuffle them.

- Place the cards face down in a stack.

- Take a card, read it and decide where to place it in the line.

		1
2	3	4
5	6	7
8	9	10

Dear Helper

This activity helps your child to read and order numbers. Begin with the cards for 1 to 5. As each card is taken, encourage your child to read it, then to place it in front of them. For each following card, ask: *Where does this card go? Why is that?* When your child is confident with reading numbers 1 to 5, extend this to nine, then include zero and ten.

Name	Date

Make ten

- ◢ You will need 20 counters or coins in a bag.

- ◢ Play this game with a friend.

- ◢ Take turns to take a handful of counters.

- ◢ Count how many you have.

- ◢ If you have ten, put a cross in your box.

- ◢ The first person to have five crosses wins the game.

Name	Name

Dear Helper
This game helps your child to count how many. It will also help your child to estimate more accurately. If your child finds counting up to ten objects difficult, limit the count to five, then, over time, extend the count to six, seven, eight, nine, ten. Encourage your child to put the counters out in front of them and to count by touching. Challenge your child to play this game again, this time taking more than ten: 11, 12, 13... up to 20 counters.

Sorting 2

- Cut out the pictures.

- Place them face-up on the table.

- Now decide how to sort the cards.

- Put them into sets.

- Tell your Helper why you have sorted them in this way.

- Can you find another way to sort the pictures?

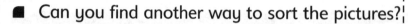

Dear Helper
This activity helps your child to sort items into sets. Talk about each picture and encourage your child to suggest what goes together. They could, for example, put all the vehicles with three, four... wheels into sets; or put all the vehicles with up to four wheels in one set and the other vehicles in another set. Ask: *How did you sort these? Is there another way?*

Challenge your child to sort some toys, telling you different ways in which they could be sorted, such as by colour, use and so on.

PHOTOCOPIABLE

www.scholastic.co.uk

NNS OBJECTIVES 🖳 Teacher's notes

Activity name	Learning objectives	Content of homework	Managing the homework	All New 100 Maths Lessons Year 2	
				NNS	Page
Ordering numbers	● Order a given set of numbers.	This is a game for two players, which involves ordering numbers.	**Before:** Using a large set of 1 to 10 cards, give these to ten children and invite the others to place the children in order. **After:** Discuss the strategies that the children used to recognise the ordering. Did they count on/back one from the card in their hands? Some children will by now just 'know' the order. Please praise these children!	1	157
Dot-to-dot	● **Recognise numerals 1 to 9.**	Some simple dot-to-dot puzzles, in which the numbers need to be joined in order to reveal four different pictures.	**Before:** Explain the activity to the children and that it is important to join the dots in order. **After:** Ask: *Which was the last number to be joined in the picture?* How do you know that?	2	163
Number search	● Begin to record numbers, initially by making marks, progressing to simple tallying and writing numerals.	The children have to search for numbers at home, such as on packets, the page number of a book or on the clock. They write down the numbers that they find and read them to their Helpers.	**Before:** Discuss where children might find numbers at home, such as page numbers in a book; the cooker clock... **After:** Invite individual children to write one of their numbers onto the flipchart for the others to see. Encourage the others to make the number in the air with large arm movements.	2	163
Coin patterns	● **Talk about, recognise and recreate simple patterns.**	The children use coins to copy simple patterns on the sheet. They discuss their patterns with the Helper, and predict what will come next in the pattern.	**Before:** Using an A3 enlarged copy of the sheet discuss the patterns that the children can see. **After:** Invite a child to make a pattern with two 1p, 2p and 5p coins. Discuss how the pattern could be changed.	3	168
How many will fit?	● Make simple estimates and predictions: for example, of the number of cubes that will fit in a box or strides across the room.	The children estimate how many cars will fit in a garage, dolls in a dolls' house, play people in an aeroplane... they then check by fitting the toys inside.	**Before:** Explain the activity to the children and, where a child has none of the suggested items, discuss what they could use instead, such as a shoebox and small toys. **After:** Carry out the activity with the children, using one of the suggested scenarios. Encourage the children to make their estimates and to explain their thinking.	3	170

NNS OBJECTIVES 📄 Teacher's notes

Activity name	Learning objectives	Content of homework	Managing the homework	All New 100 Maths Lessons Year R	
				NNS	Page
Writing numbers	● Begin to record numbers, initially by making marks, progressing to simple tallying and writing numerals.	The children count groups of cars and write how many.	**Before:** Practise with the children writing large numerals in the air with big arm movements. **After:** Ask the children to sit in pairs. One child 'writes' a given numeral onto the other's back, gently using a finger. Then the swap over.	4	175
Heavier and lighter	● **Use language such as more or less, longer or shorter, heavier or lighter... to compare two quantities.**	The children choose two items at a time from around the house and decide by holding them in their hands which is lighter and which is heavier. They record by drawing the items.	**Before:** Pass some toys around, in pairs, for the children to compare their weight by holding. Check their estimates with a balance. **After:** Invite children to say which toys they chose and which was lighter/heavier. Where another child had different results talk about how both sets are correct as the toys were probably not of the same of the same weight.	4	177
Count how many	● **Recognise numerals 1 to 9**.	Children count how many are in the pictures, and join the pictures to the numerals.	**Before:** Put out some toys. Invite a child to count how many and to find the appropriate numeral card. Repeat this for other sets. **After:** Using an A3 enlargement of the sheet, point to a set, then ask the children to draw, in the air, the appropriate numeral.	5	184
Playing shops	● Sort coins, including the £1 and £2 coins, and use them in role-play to pay and to give change.	With their Helper, children exchange a coin for an item, saying how much the coin is worth.	**Before:** Show the children the coins 1p, 2p, 5p, 10p, £1 and £2. Ask the children to name and describe the coins. **After:** Repeat the activity on the sheet using the class shop. Encourage the children to name and describe the coin/s they choose each time.	5	185
How many?	● Estimate a number in the range that can be counted reliably, then check by counting.	The children take a small handful of bricks and guess how many they have, then check by counting.	**Before:** Demonstrate the activity to the children. Ask a child to take a handful of bricks, estimate how many, then count them. **After:** With all the children repeat the activity using bricks, cubes, counting toys... Discuss how with different sized items the amount picked up will not be the same.	7	189

NNS OBJECTIVES 🗋 Teacher's notes

Activity name	Learning objectives	Content of homework	Managing the homework	All New 100 Maths Lessons Year R	
				NNS	Page
In a line	● Begin to understand and use ordinal numbers in different contexts.	The children put some toys in a line, and their Helper asks questions about their ordinal number position.	**Before:** Ask six children to stand in a line. Ask questions about them using ordinal vocabulary, such as: *Who is between the 2nd and 4th person?* **After:** Repeat the above activity, this time extending to up to 10 children. Alternately, use toys in a line instead of children.	7	189
Count in twos	● Count in twos.	The children say number rhymes that count in twos with their Helper.	**Before:** Say the rhymes through with the children several times so that they begin to join in. **After:** Repeat the rhymes with the children. Encourage them to show how many using their fingers. Repeat over time.	8	195
Total 5	● Select two groups of objects to make a given total.	The children use a piece of string to partition a set of five objects. They say the addition sentence and repeat for other partitions.	**Before:** Ask four children to stand at the front of the class. Now say: *How can we separate these children into two groups?* Try different ways and say the addition sentence each time. **After:** Ask the children to explain the different partitions they found for five.	8	197
Where is it?	● Use everyday words to describe position.	The children discuss where things are in the picture, using position words.	**Before:** Play I-Spy in the classroom so that the children can listen carefully to the vocabulary of position. **After:** Using an A3 copy of the sheet invite the children to explain where things are in the picture.	9	202
Cut and sort	● Sort and match objects, pictures or children themselves, justifying the decisions made.	Children cut out the pictures, then sort them into sets that they choose for themselves.	**Before:** Put out a selection of toys and ask the children to suggest different ways of sorting these. **After:** Ask the children to explain how they sorted the cards on the sheet, using A3 enlarged versions for all to see.	9	205
How many monsters?	● Begin to record numbers, initially by making marks, progressing to simple tallying and writing numerals.	Children count how many monsters can be found in each picture and then write the numbers in a box	**Before:** Practise drawing numerals in the air. **After:** Say a number. Ask the children to draw that numeral onto their partner's back. They swap over roles each time.	10	209

NNS OBJECTIVES ▭ Teacher's notes

Activity name	Learning objectives	Content of homework	Managing the homework	All New 100 Maths Lessons Year R	
				NNS	Page
What time is it?	● Begin to read o'clock time.	The children look at the clocks on the sheet and read the time. They begin to tell o'clock times at home.	**Before:** Using a teaching clock set it to o'clock times for the children to read. **After:** Challenge the children to tell you when the class clock 'says' an o'clock time.	10	213
Collect 5p	● **Use developing mathematical ideas and methods to solve practical problems involving counting and comparing in a real or role-play context.**	A game for two players who take it in turns to roll a dice then move on a track. The players collect coins as they go. The first one to collect 5p wins. The coins are 1p and 2p coins, so that the child finds ways of making 5p from the coins.	**Before:** Discuss how many pennies make 2p and 5p. **After:** Play the game as a class activity with an A3 enlarged sheet, and coins Blu-Tacked to it. Children take turns to remove the coin and to say what the total is.	11	220
Toss and count	● Begin to record numbers, initially by making marks, progressing to simple tallying and writing numerals.	The children toss a counter onto a grid. They count how many pictures are under the place where the counter lands, then they write the number for this.	**Before:** Toss a large spot dice. Invite a child to count the spots and write the numeral onto the flipchart. **After:** Using an A3 enlargement of the sheet, invite the children to count the pictures that you point to and draw the numeral in the air.	11	216

Ordering numbers

- This is a game for two players.

- You will need two suits of cards: Ace (1) to 10 from a pack of playing cards.

- Shuffle the cards and place them in a stack, face-down on the table.

- Take turns to take a card and hold it in your hands.

- When you have three cards in order, place these down on the table.

- You may also add to the cards on the table if you pick up a card that will continue the order.

- The winning player is the one who is first to put down all their cards.

- If it is not possible for either of you to win, the player with the least cards left in their hands is the winner.

Dear Helper

This game helps your child to order the numbers from one to ten. If your child finds this game hard, play the game with the hands of cards placed face up on the table. This way you can discuss which cards your child has and whether any of them make an ordered run of three cards. This game can be played with up to four players if all four suits of 1 to 10 cards from a pack are used.

Name

Date

Dot-to-dot

■ Join the dots in number order.

3

2   4   2   3

4

5

1   6

1   5

5

2   3   3   4   6

4   5   7

2

8

7   6   10

1   8   1   9

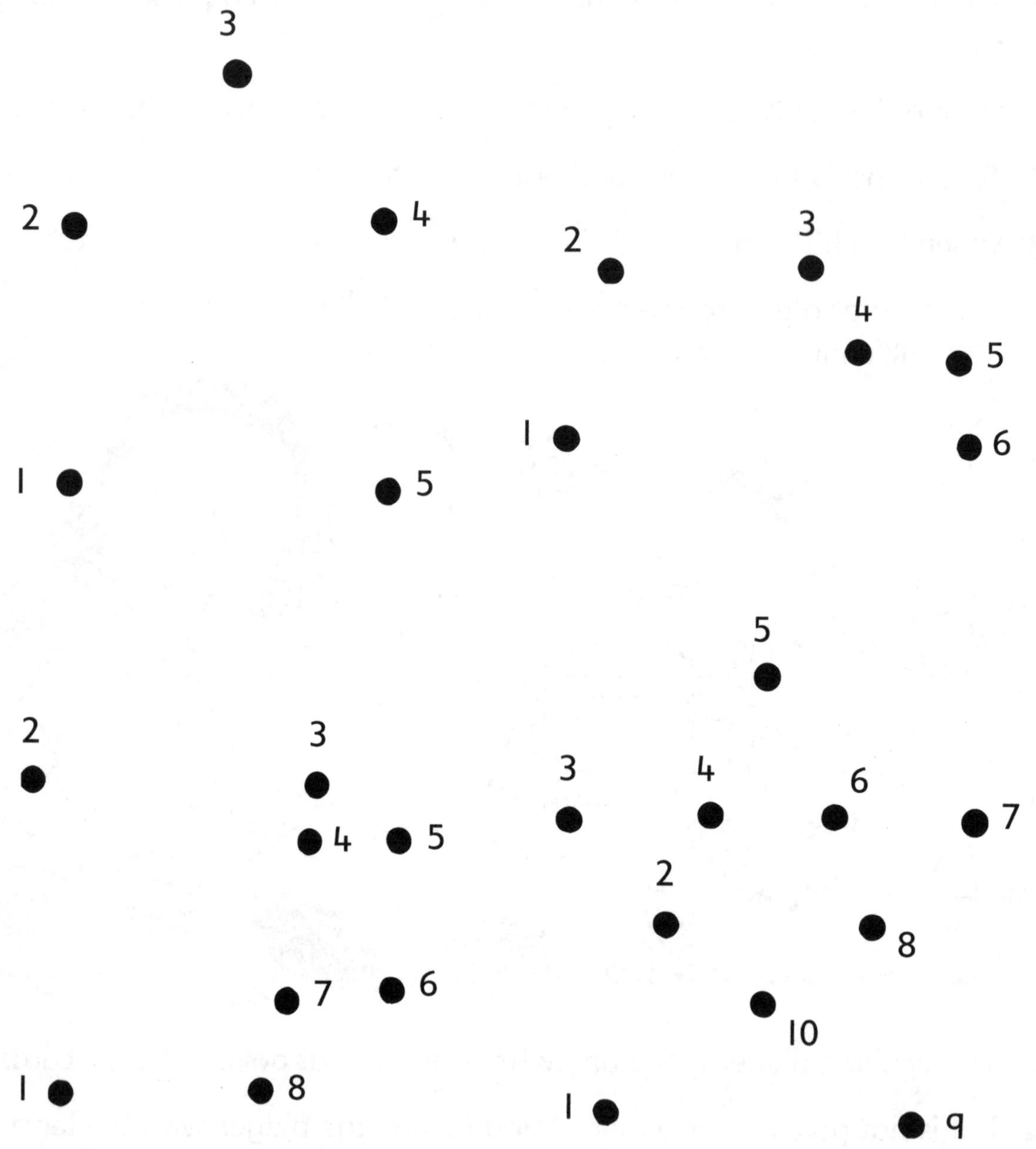

Dear Helper

This activity helps your child to read numbers. The pictures can be completed by joining the dots in number order. If your child finds this difficult, say the numbers together, in number order, and ask your child to point to each one in turn.

Challenge your child to make up their own dot-to-dot picture on the back of this sheet.

PHOTOCOPIABLE

www.scholastic.co.uk

Name _____   Date _____

Number search

- Look around you at home.

- What numbers can you see?

- Draw where the numbers are.

- Write the numbers that you can see.

Dear Helper
This activity helps your child to read and write numbers. Look together for numbers. These could be on the clock, on the television screen, from a book, or on a packet. When your child has found a number that they can read, ask them to draw where the number is to be found. Then encourage them to write the number, starting at the top of it.

Challenge your child to find numbers larger than ten, and to write these on the back of the sheet.

Coin patterns

- You will need six 1p coins, four 2p coins and four 5p coins.

- Use the coins to copy the patterns.

Dear Helper
This activity helps your child to recognise and copy patterns. Ask your child to look at the first pattern and to say what the coins are. Ask them to match the coins using real coins and to place the coins in the same pattern on the table. If your child finds this difficult, suggest that they match the coins on the sheet, placing the real coin on the picture of the coin. Ask your child to say what comes next... and next... in the pattern.

Challenge your child to spot the symmetrical pattern (it is the third one). Ask them to use a small mirror to show you that it is symmetrical.

Coins © The Royal Mint

How many will fit?

- You will need one of these:
  - garage and some cars
  - dolls' house and dolls, furniture...
  - play people and a bus, aeroplane or something similar.

- How many toys do you think will fit inside?

- Make a guess.

- Now check by counting how many will fit.

Dear Helper

This activity helps your child to make estimates and to check by counting. Ask your child to make a guess of how many will fit inside. Then ask them to check by counting. If your child makes a wild guess, talk about how much room there is and ask them to make another guess. This activity can be repeated for other things, such as how many cups of water will fit in the teapot, how many bricks will go in the box and so on.

Name

Date

Writing numbers

- Count the cars.

- Write how many.

Dear Helper
This activity helps your child to count how many and then to write the number for that quantity. If your child finds writing the numbers difficult, suggest that they draw the number in the air. Challenge your child to draw some sets of pictures, up to nine, on the back of this sheet, and write how many.

Name

Date

Heavier and lighter

- Choose two toys.

- Hold them in your hands.

- Decide which is heavier and which is lighter.

- Draw them on the balance.

- Do this two more times.

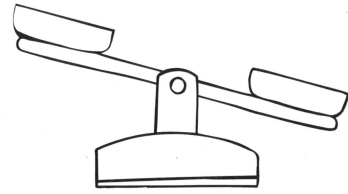

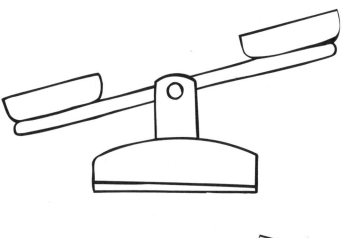

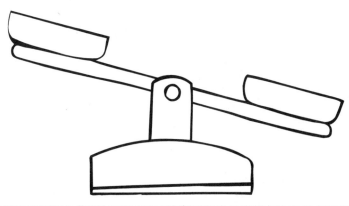

Dear Helper

This activity encourages your child to estimate for weight. Suggest that your child begins with pairs of toys that are clearly different in weight. Ask your child to draw the lighter toy on the lighter side of the balance. If they find this difficult, talk about what happens to the balance when things are put onto it. If necessary, remind your child that the balance will show the heavier toy as 'down' and the lighter toy as 'up'.

Challenge your child to try to find two toys that they think weigh about the same. Ask them to draw their own balance for this, which should show the two pans level.

Name   Date

Count how many

- Count how many in the picture.
- Join the picture to its number.

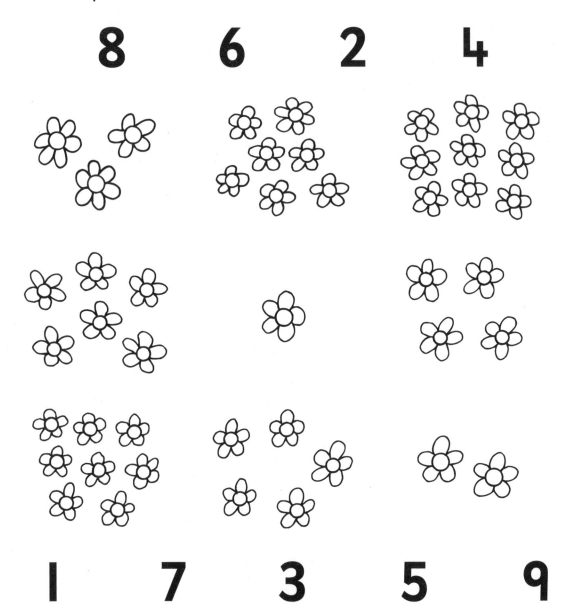

8   6   2   4

1   7   3   5   9

Dear Helper
This activity helps your child to count how many and to recognise the numeral. Begin by asking your child to count the pictures in one of the groups, and then ask your child to find the matching numeral. If your child finds this difficult, rewrite the numbers one to nine along the bottom of the sheet, in number order. Ask: *Which number do we want?* Help your child to count along the numbers until they come to the one that matches the chosen picture.
   Challenge your child to draw more pictures, with amounts up to ten, and to write the numerals.

Playing shops

- You will need one each of 1p, 2p, 5p, 10p, 20p, 50p, £1 and £2 coins.

- Find some things to use as a shop.

- Ask your Helper to work with you.

- Your Helper will tell you how much something in the shop costs.

- Give your Helper that coin.

Dear Helper

This activity helps your child to sort and name all the coins. Say, for example: *This toy car costs £2.*
Check to see if your child can recognise and give you the £2 coin. If your child finds this difficult, ask
your child to find the 1p coin, 2p coin, and so on. These can then be laid in order of value. Talk about
the differences in size and colour between the coins until your child is confident with recognising and
naming them.

 Challenge your child to give you other amounts, combining coins, such as £3, 3p and 7p.

Name

Date

How many?

- You will need some bricks.

- Take a handful of bricks.

- Guess how many you have.

- Write that number.

- Now count them.

- Write that number.

- Did you make a good guess?

- Do this three more times.

My guess ☐   My guess ☐   My guess ☐   My guess ☐

My count ☐   My count ☐   My count ☐   My count ☐

Dear Helper
This activity helps your child to improve their estimation skills. Small toys other than bricks can be used, as long as the maximum total picked up is ten or less. If your child makes inaccurate guesses, encourage them to repeat this activity at least six times. Each time ask: *How many do you think there are? How many have you counted?*

Challenge your child to use something smaller, such as some coins, and to estimate and count quantities up to about 20.

In a line

- Cut out these pictures of toys.

- Put the pictures in a line in front of you.

- Ask your Helper to ask you some questions about them.

Dear Helper

This activity helps your child to use the language of ordinal number: first, second, third and so on. First, help your child to cut out the pictures. Ask questions about them, such as: *Which toy is first, second, third...? Which toy is between the third and the fifth?* Then suggest that your child moves one of the pictures to make that one the first or third. If your child finds this difficult, count the pictures together each time so that your child recognises which number position they need to consider.

Challenge your child to repeat this activity with ten or fifteen pictures. You could use real toys.

Count in twos

■ Say these rhymes with your Helper.

Mary at the garden gate
Mary at the garden gate
Two, four, six, eight,
Mary at the garden gate,
Eating cherries off a plate.

Anon, from *Early Years Poems and Rhymes*
compiled by Jill Bennett, (1993) Scholastic Ltd.

Ten crafty crocodiles
*Invite your child to place hands together as if in prayer and then lock fingers
together. They can tuck two fingers down inside palms with each verse.*

Ten crafty crocodiles cooped up in a crate
Two crept out and then there were eight.

Eight crafty crocodiles broke the crate to bits
Two crept out and then there were six.

Six crafty crocodiles crashed the crate's door
Two crept out and then there were four.

Four crafty crocodiles with nothing else to do
Two crept away and then there were two.

 Two crafty crocodiles now the crate had gone
Crept along the riverside and then there were none.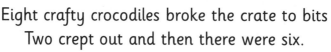

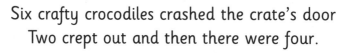

Neela Mann and Brenda Williams

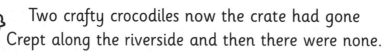

Dear Helper
You child has been learning to count in twos. Say the first rhyme through together several times.
Ask your child to hold up the appropriate number of fingers for each number that they say. Then
encourage your child to say the rhyme on their own. Repeat this for the second rhyme which counts
back in twos.

When your child is confident with these rhymes, suggest that they teach them to someone else.

PHOTOCOPIABLE

www.scholastic.co.uk

Total five

- You will need a piece of string.

- Put the string down on the sheet.

- Separate the animals using the string.

- Say how many animals there are on one side of the string.

- Say how many animals there are on the other side of the string.

- Say an addition sentence for the animals.

- Find three more ways to do this.

Dear Helper

This activity helps your child to realise that there are different ways of making the same total.
The totals for five are: 0, 5; 1, 4; 2, 3; 3, 2; 4, 1; 5, 0. At this stage your child will probably think, for example, that one add four is different from four add one.
If your child finds this difficult, put the string down to separate the five animals into four and one and ask: *How many here? And how many here? How many are there altogether?* Then say the addition sentence: one add four makes five altogether.

 Challenge your child to draw some more animals and say addition sentences for other numbers, up to about ten.

Where is it?

- Ask your Helper to work with you.

- Your Helper will ask you where things are in the picture.

Dear Helper

This activity helps your child to use words about position. Look at the picture and ask your child questions about things in the picture.

    For example, point to a child and ask: *Where is this child?* If your child finds this hard, ask questions such as: *Which child is on the swing?* so that your child can point.

PHOTOCOPIABLE

Cut and sort

- Cut out the pictures.

- Decide how to sort the pictures.

- Show your Helper what you have done.

- Can you find another way to sort the pictures?

Dear Helper

This activity helps your child to make decisions about how to sort. For these pictures, your child might sort out the puppies, adult dogs, kittens and adult cats. Or, your child might put adults in one group and baby animals in the other. Ask your child to explain to you how they have sorted the pictures. If your child finds this activity hard, try suggesting a way to start, such as sorting out the puppies.

Challenge your child to find different ways to sort the pictures.

Name   Date

How many monsters?

- Count how many.
- Write the number.

Dear Helper
This activity helps your child to write numbers. Watch as your child writes how many and if necessary, remind them of the direction of the number, always starting at the top. If your child finds it hard to write the number, practise drawing it in the air with large arm movements.
   Challenge your child to write the numerals 0 to 10 in order.

PHOTOCOPIABLE

www.scholastic.co.uk

What time is it?

◼ Look at these clocks.

◼ Say the times.

Dear Helper
This activity helps your child to begin to tell the time. At this stage your child will be learning to tell the time with a clock with hands (analogue clock) rather than a digital clock. Look at the clocks *together and ask questions such as: Where is the minute (big) hand pointing? Where is the hour (little) hand pointing? So what time is it?*

Encourage your child to begin to tell the time during the course of the day. For example, if you are all going out at 10 o'clock, say: *Tell me when it is 10 o'clock.*

As a challenge, encourage your child to look at the clocks around the house and to begin to say the time.

Collect 5p

- You will need:
  - five 1p and five 2p coins
  - a 1–6 dice
  - a counter for each player.

- Ask your Helper to play this game with you.

- Take turns to roll the dice.

- Move your counter the number shown on the dice.

- If you land on a coin then collect the matching coin.

- The first person to collect 5p wins the game.

Dear Helper

This activity helps your child to recognise that a 2p coin is worth two 1p coins. Play this game together. If your child finds the game hard, begin with all 1p coins on the track. Then, when your child has collected 5p, talk together about how two of the 1p coins are worth the same as a 2p coin. Change four 1p coins for two 2p coins and discuss how this is still worth 4p.

Challenge your child to play the game again, this time collecting 10p, and substitute some 5p coins for 1p coins.

Name _____   Date _____

Toss and count

- You will need:
  - a counter or penny
  - a pencil.

- Toss a counter onto the grid.

- Count the pictures where the counter lands.

- Write the number in the box.

- Do this five more times.

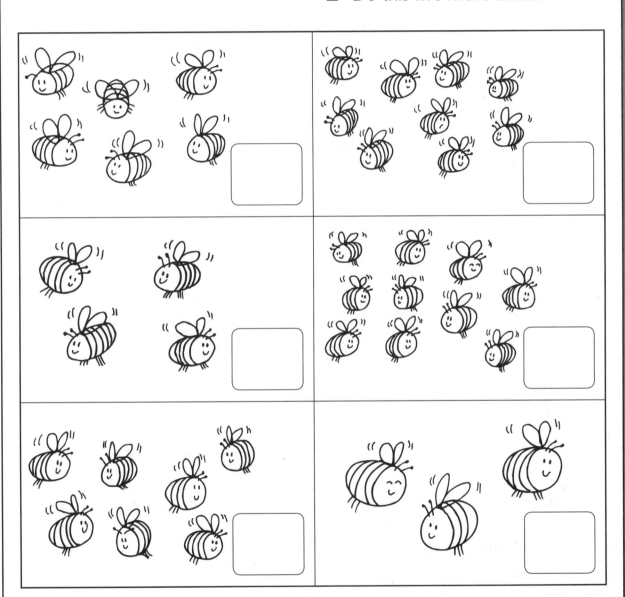

Dear Helper
This activity helps your child to count, then write the number. Ask: *How many did you count?* Check by counting a different way. Watch your child count and check that they count all of the pictures in the square each time. If your child finds this hard, suggest that they touch each one, in turn, working from one side of the square to the other.

PHOTOCOPIABLE

www.scholastic.co.uk

ALL NEW 100 MATHS HOMEWORK AND ASSESSMENT • YEAR R

Key objectives in Reception year

Below is the complete list of key objectives covered in Reception. The letters alongside each objective also appear in the assessment overviews.

a Say and use the number names in order in familiar contexts.

b Count reliably up to 10 everyday objects.

c Recognise numerals 1 to 9.

d Use language such as more or less, greater or smaller, longer or shorter, heavier or lighter, to compare two numbers or quantities.

e In practical activities and discussion, begin to use the vocabulary involved in adding and subtracting.

f Find one more or one less than a number from 1 to 10.

g Begin to relate addition and subtraction to combining two groups of objects, and subtraction to 'taking away'.

h Talk about, recognise and recreate simple patterns.

i Use language such as circle or bigger to describe the shape and size of solids and flat shapes.

j Use everyday words to describe position.

k Use developing mathematical ideas and methods to solve practical problems.

About the assessment units

The planning for the assessment units is based upon the NNS medium-term plans and the Curriculum Guidance for the Foundation Stage (DfEE, 1999). There is an assessment unit for each end of half-term, as well as end of year assessments.

For each assessment unit, there are two detailed lesson plans, one for each Key objective that is assessed at this half-term point, with an accompanying photocopiable activity sheet for each lesson.

The lesson plans include oral and mental starters, practical and written activities as well as suggestions for further support.

The end-of-year assessment consists of two separate assessments, which cover all the Key objectives taught during the year. These are set within the play contexts of 'In the café' and 'The sand tray'.

Using the assessment units

Choose the half-term assessment that matches your planning. From your ongoing teacher assessment, identify the children who have already achieved specific Key objectives. Now decide which are the children who you suspect may have achieved the Key objective/s but for whom you have no firm assessment data. These children can form the target group for assessment and can work with an adult during practical activities. The adult should use the probing questions included in the assessment notes for teachers.

The assessment activities are mainly practical and for small groups of children. Most of the assessment lessons have a photocopiable 'Help sheet' for adults to follow. These help sheets include spaces for recording the outcomes of the assessment.

During the Reception year at school there will be some children working towards the blue and green Stepping Stones found in the Curriculum guidance for the Foundation Stage (QCA). There are grids for each term available which contain the Stepping Stone statements (blue and green for Term 1, and green for Terms 2 and 3) as well as suggested probing questions to ask while the children are engaged in mathematical activities. The outcomes of these can be used to make decisions about the next steps for these children.

Supporting teaching assistants in using the activities

Decide which group the teaching assistant should support. Provide details of the activity (practical or written) and discuss the probing questions to be used. Talk about how to observe and record details of the children's responses.

Take time to discuss the outcomes of the assessment activity together. Make notes about individual children. These notes will be useful in forward planning.

Assessment for learning

Assessment is always for a purpose, and in this case, it is to check what specific children understand, know and can do, and where they need further teaching in order to achieve the Key objectives. Use the outcomes of the assessment for forward planning, for teaching and for homework provision.

Assess and Review

Key objectives to be assessed
Assessment lesson 1: **Say and use the number names in familiar contexts.**
Assessment lesson 2: **Use language such as 'circle' or 'bigger' to describe the shape and size of solids and flat shapes.**

Photocopiable pages
'Count the animals' sheet for each child (page 83); copy of 'Help sheet for shape' for adult Helpers (page 85); 'Work mat 1' (page 86)

Equipment
Set of 2D and 3D shapes, a feely box or bag; ten toys for counting; basket with items from the dressing up box for comparing lengths of scarves etc.

Assessment Activities

Mental maths assessment

1. Number names a
Ask groups of children to say the number names from one to five initially. Repeat to ten. Then, ask the children to say the number names, in order, around the group. Repeat this several times, starting with a different child each time.
Probing questions
● *Why do we have to say the number names in the same order each time?*
● *Listen to me count: one, two, four, five... Is that correct? What did I do wrong?*

2. One more than... f
Invite groups of children to put ten counting toys onto the table. Now place five of them in a line. Say: *How many toys can you see? What if I put one more on the table? How many would there be now?* Invite children to say how many, then check by adding one more and counting again. Repeat this for different quantities, from one to five initially, then extending to nine toys.
Probing questions
● *How many toys are there?*
● *How many would there be if I put in one more?*

Practical maths assessment
1. Counting objects b
Give each pair ten counting toys and a copy of 'Work mat 1' (page 86). Say a number of toys and ask the children to count out this number on the mat, eg *Put three toys on the mat.* Repeat for several different amounts - first to five, then if the children are confident, extend this to ten. Check your result.

Probing questions
● *How can you be sure that all of the toys have been counted?*
● *Watch me count these.* (Count up to six toys, but repeat a number in the counting sequence). *What have I done wrong? Can you count them for me?*

2. Longer and shorter d
Put out a basket of items and invite children to choose two items each. Ask them to compare the two items and say which is longer or shorter. Observe the activity and check that they understand that to make careful comparisons they should match one end of each and compare the other ends. Repeat for different pairs of items (scarves, socks etc.)
Probing questions
● *Which is longer? Which is shorter? How can you tell?*
● *Use these two things (items that are close, but not the same, in length). Show me how you can find out which is longer or shorter.*

WEEK 6 LESSON 1 Half-term assessment

Number names

Key objective
Say and use the number names in familiar contexts.

What you need
● A copy of activity sheet 'Count the animals' (page 83) for each child
● an A3 enlargement of 'Count the animals' (page 83).

Further support
● Ask an adult to work with children who need support with counting.
● The sets of animals in the top half of the sheet of 'Count the animals' are smaller than in the bottom half of the sheet.
● Using the A3 enlargement of 'Count the animals', folded so that just the top half shows, ask the adult to invite a child to touch and count a set of animals while the other children watch.
● If the children find this difficult, then the adult can point to each animal in turn while the children say the counting names.

Oral and mental starter

Sing a counting rhyme for numbers to five, such as *Five little speckled frogs.* Invite the children to take turns to do the actions for this. If children are confident with numbers to five, then increase the number of frogs to six, seven and so on.

Main assessment activity

Explain that today you would like the children to use the counting numbers as they work. Pin the A3 enlargement of 'Count the animals' to the flipchart. Ask *How many dogs can you see? How many cats...?* Invite a child to come to the flipchart and to count the animals and check that they coordinate the touch and count.

Ask the children to work in small groups of three or four. Each child will need a copy of 'Count the animals'. They take turns to choose one of the groups of animals and count these.
As the children work ask questions such as:
● *How many ___ are there?*
● *How do you know that?*
● *Can you show me a different way to count them?*
● *Why do we have to say the number names in the same order when we count?*

Plenary

Using the A3 enlargement of 'Count the animals', invite the children to suggest which group of animals has four/six/seven members. Invite a child to come to the flipchart and to check by touching and counting.

Possible difficulties	Next steps
Does not say the number names in order.	Give further experience of saying and singing number rhymes with numbers up to five initially, then extend the count over time.

Count the animals

Shape

Key objective
Use language such as circle or bigger to describe the shape and size of solids and flat shapes.

What you need
● A set of 3D shapes including cubes, cones, pyramids and spheres.
● a set of 2D shape tiles including squares, triangles, circles, rectangles and stars
● a feely box or opaque bag.
● copy of 'Help sheet for Shape' (page 85) for adult Helpers.

Further support
● Where children are unsure about shapes, their properties and their names, put another set of shapes in view of the children so that they can refer to these as a reminder of what individual shapes look like.

Oral and mental starter
Put some 3D shapes into the feely box or bag and ask the children to sit in a circle. Explain that you will pass the box around the circle. When you say: *Stop!* ask the child with the box to find the shape that you say. The child finds the shape and brings it out of the box for all to check if they agree. Keep the pace of this sharp. You may like to use a tape of some music as the box is being passed around the group.

Main assessment activity
Work with a small group of about four children and begin with the 3D shapes, putting these into the box in front of the children so that they see each shape go inside. Keep one of each shape out on the table for all to see. Ask the children to pass the box and take it in turns to feel for a shape. Now ask questions of the first child such as:
● *Does your shape have flat faces?*
● *Does your shape have any curves?*

Encourage the other children to guess what the shape might be. If they cannot name it ask them to point to the shape. Then check by asking the child with the box to show the shape.
Repeat this for each child to have a turn.

This activity can be repeated for 2D shape tiles in the same way. Questions could include:
● *Does your shape have straight sides?*
● *Are all the sides the same length?*

Ask probing questions such as:
● *I shall hide a shape. Listen. Can you guess which shape I have?*
● *Now you find a shape and hide it. Tell me what you can feel. Can I guess what it is?*

Plenary
Repeat the starter, this time with flat shapes. Again, keep the pace sharp. You may choose to target specific children as the box is passed around the circle, so that those for whom you are not sure about their confidence with 2D shapes can be checked.

Possible difficulties	Next steps
Children may confuse 3D and 2D shapes, such as calling a cube a square, a sphere a circle...	Provide further experiences of naming and exploring the properties of both 3D and 2D shapes. Encourage the child to see how, for example, a cube has square faces, by printing with a cube.

Help sheet for Shape

You will need
- A set of 3D shapes including cubes, cones, pyramids and spheres
- a set of 2D shape tiles including squares, triangles, circles, rectangles and stars
- a feely box or opaque bag.

Work with a small group of about four children and begin with the 3D shapes, putting these into the box in front of the children so that they see each shape go inside. Keep one of each shape out on the table for all to see. Ask the children to pass the box and take it in turns to feel for a shape. Now ask questions of the first child such as:
- Does your shape have flat faces?
- Does your shape have any curves?

Encourage the other children to guess what the shape might be. If they cannot name it ask them to point to the shape. Then check by asking the child with the box to show the shape.

Repeat this until each child has had a turn. The activity can be repeated for 2D shape tiles in the same way.

Ask probing questions such as:
- I shall hide a shape. Can you guess which shape I have?
- Now you find a shape and hide it. Tell me what you can feel. Is it a ___?

Record the children's achievements.

Child's name	Demonstrated confidence	Had difficulties

Work mat 1

PHOTOCOPIABLE

www.scholastic.co.uk

Assess and Review

Key objectives to be assessed
Assessment lesson 1: **Count reliably up to 10 everyday objects.**
Assessment lesson 2: **Find one more or one less than a number from 1 to 10.**

Photocopiable pages
'Work mat 2' (page 89) for each child; 'Help sheet for Finding one more or one less' (page 91) for each adult helper; '2D shape tiles' (page 92)

such as cubes, spheres, cones, pyramids; cubes in three different colours; bucket balance; parcels in different weights and sizes; six teddies; six chairs; a large cake and a table.

Equipment
Ten counting toys for each child; 3D shapes

Assessment Activities

Mental maths assessment
Count to ten b
Ask a group of six to eight children to count together to ten. Encourage them to keep the pace sharp by swinging their arms or, gently, punching the air. Repeat, this time by asking the children to count around the group. Do this several times, and each time ask a different child to begin on one.
Probing questions
● *Why do we have to say the numbers in the same order when we count?*

Practical maths assessment
1. Patterns h
Put out alternating red and blue cubes and ask a group of children: *What is the pattern? What comes next?* Invite the children to add to the pattern. Now repeat this for a more complex pattern, such as an AABAAB pattern. Now ask the children to shut their eyes. Remove a piece from the pattern and say: *Open your eyes. Look at the pattern. What do you see?* Encourage the children to explain what has happened.
Probing questions
● *What is special about how I have ordered these cubes?*
● *What is wrong with this pattern?*

2. 3D/2D shape sort i
Put out a selection of 3D shapes onto the table and invite the children in a group of four to sort them into sets. Say: *Put all the cubes together.*

Check that they are beginning to use the vocabulary of 3D shape. Repeat for sets of 2D shapes taken from the '2D shape tiles' sheet
Probing questions
● *What shape is this? How do you know that?*
● *Tell me something special about a ___*

3. Heavier and lighter d
Ask a group of children to compare two parcels by holding them, and then check using a balance. Check that they understand how to interpret the positions of the buckets. Repeat for other parcels.
Probing questions
● *Which do you think is heavier/lighter? How can you tell? How can we check?*
● *What does the balance show you?*

4. Solving problems k
Put out four teddies on chairs around the table, and have another two teddies to hand. Ask *How many teddies are there at the table? How many chairs are there? Here are some more teddies. How many are there? So, how many chairs will we need for these teddies? How many teddies are there altogether? And how many chairs?* Repeat this for a plate of play food, encouraging the children to share out the food and decide whether there is enough.
Probing questions
● *Are there enough chairs for the teddies? How many more do we need?*
● *How many cakes do we need so that each teddy can have one?*

Counting

What you need
● Opaque bag with some counting toys in it
● copies of activity sheet 'Work mat 2' (page 89)
● pots or trays of counting toys for each pair of children.

Further support
● Where children are not confident yet with counting to ten, reduce the number of items to be counted to up to four... five... six. Ask an adult to work with these children. The adult should check the children's method of counting:
  ● Do they coordinate touching the toy (perhaps moving it) and saying the number name?
  ● Do they count one at a time with the numbers in counting order?
  ● Do they stop the count on the last item?
  ● Do they recognise that the last number said dictates how many in the set?

Oral and mental starter
Put out five toys in a line for all the children to see. Explain that you will point to the toys and ask the children to count them as you point. Repeat this several times for different quantities of toys from one to ten.

Main assessment activity
Ask the children to sit in a circle. Explain that you will pass a bag with some toys in it around the circle. When you say: *Stop!*, ask the child who is holding the bag to take out a given number of toys. For example, say: *Zoe, take out five toys.* Check that the child has an appropriate counting strategy for taking out the toys, such as counting out one at a time, or tipping out the toys, then separating out the required number. Repeat this several times, each time asking the other children: *How many have been counted out? Who will check this for me?* Finally, each time, ask the child with the bag to count the toys, aloud, back into the bag.

Now provide each child with a copy of activity sheet 'Work mat 2'. This is a sheet which has a space for counting out toys onto it. Ask the children to work in pairs. They take turns to say a number between one and ten. The other child counts out that number of toys onto their work mat, then their partner checks the count.

As the children work, ask questions such as:
● *How can you be sure that you have counted all the toys?*
● *Can you check in a different way?*
● *What would happen if we didn't start the count with 'one'?*

Plenary
Repeat the activity with the bag and toys from the beginning of the Main assessment activity. Choose different children this time to count out a given number of toys. This will give you further opportunities to assess individual children's ability with counting.

Possible difficulty	Next step
Does not say the counting numbers in order.	Practise saying the counting names in order through saying and singing counting rhymes so that the child becomes fluent with these.
Does not coordinate the touch, move and saying the counting number.	Provide more experience in touching, moving and saying the counting number. Keep the quantities small, such as four, five, six and so on until the child is confident.
Does not recognise that the last number said represents 'how many'.	Touch, move and count together, with an adult helping, and emphasis that the count stops at the last item.

Work mat 2

Finding one more or less

Key objective
Find one more or less than a number from 1 to 10.

What you need
● Photocopiable page 'Work mat 2' (page 89) for each child
● a copy of 'Help sheet for Finding one more or less' (page 91) for each adult Helper
● counting toys
● a clear container.

Further support
● Limit the size of the count, for example, up to four or five, to begin with.
● Encourage the children to count aloud how many toys they have put out then to say the next number in the count.
● Repeat this for one less than, putting out the toys, counting them, then beginning to count back in order to find one less than.

Oral and mental starter
Explain that you will say a number. Ask the children to hold up that number of fingers. Now ask them to show you the number of fingers that is one more/one less than the number that you said. Repeat this, keeping the numbers to up to five to begin with, then extending to up to ten.

Main assessment activity
Show the children the clear container. Now drop in five counting toys, one by one. Ask: *How many toys are in the jar?* Now add one more and ask *How many are in the jar now?* Repeat this, but this time, removing one toy.

This activity requires an adult with about four children. Explain that you would like the children to count out some objects onto their work mat. Say: *Put out four toys onto your mat. How many would there be if there were one more? Put one more out and check.* Repeat this for different quantities up to about ten, and for one less than.

As the children work ask probing questions such as:
● *What is one more than ___?*
● *How did you work that out?*
● *What is one less than ___?*
● *How did you work that out?*

Plenary
Invite the children to sit in a circle. Explain that you will say a number. Ask the children to count together to that number. Now say: *What is one more than ___?* Encourage the children to say the next number. Repeat this for one less than. If children are unsure about finding one more or less than a number working mentally, repeat the activity from the beginning of the Main assessment activity.

Possible difficulties	Next steps
Does not recognise the next number in a count.	Give further experience of counting, stopping the count and saying: *What is the next number?* Keep the count to up to five to begin with, then extend the count up to ten over time.
Does not recognise one less than a given number.	Give further experience of counting backwards, starting initially from three, then four, then five, and so on. When the child is confident ask *What is one less than ___?* to check that they now understand.

Help sheet for Finding one more or less

Each child will need a work mat and ten counting toys. Work with a group of about four children. Explain that you would like the children to count out some objects onto their work mat. Say: Put out four toys onto your mat. How many would there be if there was one more? Put one more out and check. Repeat this for different quantities up to about ten, and for one less than.

As the children work ask probing questions such as:

◖ What is one more than _____?
◖ How did you work that out?
◖ What is one less than _____?
◖ How did you work that out?

Record the children's achievements. It would be helpful to record which children can say one more and one less than a number to ten with confidence and which children had difficulties and what those difficulties were.

Child's name	Demonstrated confidence	Had difficulties

2D shape tiles

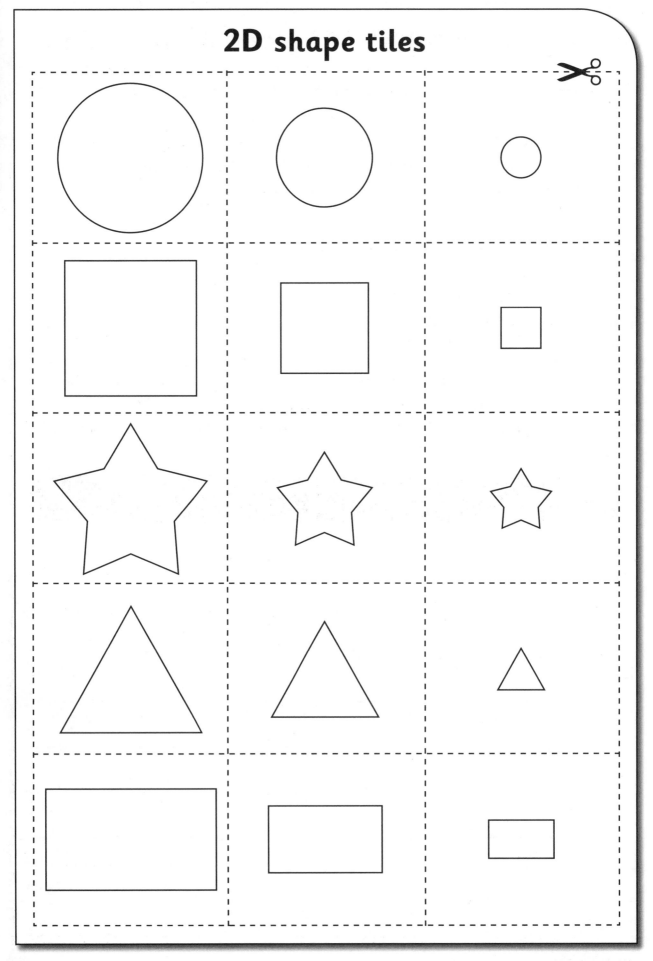

Observation grid

Decide whether to use these assessment questions during relevant units of work, or at the end of term during the 'Assess and review' activities. A section has been included to add comments for individual children.

Child's name _____ **Date** _____

Blue Stepping Stones	Probing questions	Comments
Use some number names accurately in play.	What numbers did we say in the rhyme?	
Willingly attempt to count, with some numbers in the correct order.	(Listening to the puppet count: 1, 2, 2, 3) What did the puppet do wrong? What should he say?	
Recognise groups with one, two or three objects.	(Explain that you will uncover some toys then quickly put the cover back.) How many were there?	
Show interest by sustained construction activity or by talking about shapes or arrangements. Use shapes appropriately for tasks. Begin to talk about the shapes of everyday objects.	Which shapes did you choose? Why did you choose those shapes? Which shapes are good for making ___? Why is that? Can you put some toys in this box? Which ones will fit?	
Show curiosity about numbers by offering comments or asking questions. Show an interest in number problems.	Do you think there are enough ___ for everyone to have one each? Why?	
Separate a group of three or four objects in different ways, beginning to recognise that the total is still the same.	How many ___ are there? How many ___ are there now? How do you know?	
Show confidence with numbers by initiating or requesting number activities.	How many are there? How do you know?	

AUTUMN ASSESSMENT

Observation grid

Child's name _____ Date _____

Green Stepping Stones	Probing questions	Comments
Count up to three or four objects by saying one number name for each item.	*(Listening to the puppet count: 1, 2, 3, 3, 4; 1, 2, 3, 5, 6.)* What did the puppet do wrong? What should he say?	
Find the total number of items in two groups by counting all of them.	*(Children to take two handfuls of cubes and say how many in each hand.)* How many altogether? How did you find out?	
Say with confidence the number that is one more than a given number.	If I give you one more ___ how many will you have? How do you know?	
Sustain interest for a length of time on a pre-decided construction or arrangement.

Use appropriate shapes to make representational models

Match some shapes by recognising similarities and orientation.

Show curiosity and observation by talking about shapes.

Begin to use mathematical names for 'solid' 3D shapes and 'flat' 2D shapes. | Which shapes did you choose to make this? Why are these good for building a ___? What other shapes could you choose?

What is the same/different about these two shapes?

What is this shape called? | |
| Order two or three items by length.

Adapt shapes or cut material to size. | Which do you think is longer/wider/narrower/shorter?

How can you check? How will you make this fit? | |
| Sometimes show confidence and offer solutions to problems.

Use own methods to solve a problem. | How many can we each have? How can we find out? | |
| Say the number after any number up to 9. | What comes after ___? | |

Assess and Review

Key objectives to be assessed

Assessment lesson 1: **In practical activities and discussion, begin to use the vocabulary involved in adding and subtracting.**

Assessment lesson 2: **Begin to relate subtraction to 'taking away'.**

Photocopiable pages

'Work mat 1' (page 86) or 'Work mat 2' (page 89), 'Help sheet for adding and subtracting' (page 97), 'Help sheet for taking away' (page 99), 'Counting objects record sheet' (page 100).

Equipment

Ten small counting toys in a pot for each child, glove puppet, range of different containers (eg jugs, plastic bottles, thimbles etc).

Assessment Activities

Mental maths assessment

Counting b

Explain that you would like them to count around a group. If the children gently swing their arms or punch the air as they say each number name it will help them to keep a good rhythm to the counting. Repeat the counting around the group several times, so that the children count from one, or zero, to nine or ten. Now ask the children to listen to the puppet counting. Make some errors as the puppet counts, such as omitting a word: o*ne, two, four, five...*; putting the words in the wrong order...*six, eight, seven, nine...*; repeating a word: ...*four, five, five, six....*

Probing questions

● *Why do we have to say the numbers in the same order each time?*

● *What was wrong with that count? What should it be?*

Practical maths assessment

1. How many? b

Put out the tubs of counting toys onto the table. Say: *Put out six counting toys.* Check how the children count out the toys. Now ask them to put the toys back in the tub and to take a different tub. Ask them to count out six of these toys. Invite the children to check each other's counting. Watch how they do this; do they touch and move, touch or point? A 'Counting objects record sheet' has been provided to support assessment of this and other counting activities

Probing questions

● *How can you be sure that you have counted out six?*

● *Why do we have to say the counting numbers in the same order each time?*

● *What would happen if we didn't start with one?*

2. Fill it out d

Ask pairs of children to work at the sand or water tray. Provide a range of different containers. Encourage the children to fill and pour from one container to another.

Probing questions

● *Which one holds more... less? How can you check?*

● *Which container holds more? How do you know that?*

● *Which holds less? How do you know that?*

● *About how far up this bottle* (showing a large bottle) *do you think this* (pointing to a smaller, full, container) *water will go? Why do you think that?*

Adding and subtracting vocabulary

Key objective
In practical activities and discussion, begin to use the vocabulary involved in adding and subtracting.

What you need
● Activity sheet 'Work mat 2'
● ten small counting toys for each child in a pot
● 'Help sheet for Adding and subtracting'.

Further support
● Decide whether to concentrate on quantities up to about five.
● Begin with addition and encourage the children to say the addition sentences for themselves once they have manipulated the counting toys.
● Repeat this for subtraction, using five as the maximum quantity of toys, to begin with.
● Over time, repeat this assessment, extending the quantity of toys to six... seven... up to ten.

Oral and mental starter
Ask the children to use their fingers to help them to solve the addition problems that you will say. Say, for example, *What is three add two? How many are four and one altogether? What is four and six? What is the total of four and four?* In each case ask a child to demonstrate how they solved the problem. Take note of the vocabulary that they use to respond, and check that they are beginning to use the vocabulary of addition.

Main assessment activity
Work with a group of about four children. Provide each child with a copy of 'Work mat'. Ask the children to put out the quantity of toys that you say onto their mat, then to listen carefully to what you would like them to do next. Say: *Put out four toys. Now put out another toy. How many toys have you altogether? So what is four add one?* Repeat this for other quantities, making addition sentences, such as *What is three and two? What is the total of four and one? What does five and two make?*

Repeat this for subtraction. Ask the children to put out six toys and say: *How many toys do you have on your mat? Now take away two. How many are left? So what is six take away two?* Repeat this for other subtraction sentences such as: *Take four from seven. How many are left? So what is seven take away four? What is two less than five? How many more do I need to make ___?*

Encourage the children to listen carefully and to follow the addition and subtraction instructions with their toys. Then ask the more abstract addition or subtraction question about what they have just done, such as *What is ___ add___?* Or: *What is ___ take away ___?* to check that they are beginning to understand and use the vocabulary of addition and subtraction.

Plenary
Repeat the starter, this time for the vocabulary of subtraction. Say, for example, *What is six take away two? Put up seven fingers. Now take away three. How many are left? Put up five fingers. Put down some fingers so that two are left. How many are gone? Put up eight fingers. How many more do we need to make ten?* Check each time how children solved the problem and listen to the vocabulary that they use to check that they are beginning to use and understand the vocabulary of subtraction.

Possible difficulty	Next step
Child understands some, but not all, of the vocabulary used for addition and subtraction.	Provide further practical experiences of listening to, and using, the vocabulary that is not yet understood so that the child begins to relate the vocabulary to the practical experience.

Help sheet for Adding and subtracting

You will need
◾ Ten small counting toys for each child in a pot
◾ copies of 'Work mat 2' (page 89).

Work with a group of about four children. Provide each child with a work mat. Ask the children to put out the quantity of toys that you say onto their mat, then to listen carefully to what you would like them to do next. Say: *Put out four toys. Now put out another toy. How many toys have you altogether? So what is four add one?* Repeat this for other quantities, making addition sentences, such as *What is three and two? What is the total of four and one? What does five and two make?*

Repeat this for subtraction. Ask the children to put out six toys and say: *How many toys do you have on your mat? Now take away two. How many are left? So what is six take away two?* Repeat this for other subtraction sentences such as: *Take four from seven. How many are left? So what is seven take away four? What is two less than five? How many more do I need to make ___?*

Encourage the children to listen carefully and to follow the addition and subtraction instructions with their toys. Then ask the more abstract addition or subtraction question about what they have just done, such as *What is ___ add ___?* Or *What is ___ take away ___?* to check that they are beginning to understand and use the vocabulary of addition and subtraction.

Record the children's achievements. It would be helpful to record how well the children use the vocabulary of addition and subtraction in explaining their results, and recording which vocabulary children did not yet understand or use.

Child's name	Demonstrated confidence	Had difficulties

Subtraction

Key objective
Begin to relate subtraction to 'taking away'.

What you need
● 'Help sheet for Taking away' (page 99)
● four copies of 'Work mat 2' (page 89)
● ten small counting toys in a pot for each child.

Further support
● Reduce the amounts for subtraction to starting with up to five counting toys for those who are not confident with this topic.
● Encourage the children to count out the set, then to count as they take away, and finally to count what is left.
● Put this into a sentence, for example: *four take away three leaves one.*

Oral and mental starter
Count together from zero to ten and back again. Keep the pace sharp. Then ask the children to count around the group, again keeping the pace sharp, to 10 then back to zero. Repeat this several times. If a child falters, then supply the counting number for them so that the pace is kept.

Main assessment activity
Work with a group of four children or ask an adult to carry out the activity, using 'Help sheet for Taking away'.

Ask the children to sit at a table, each with a work mat and counting toys in a pot in front of them. Explain that you will ask each child to take a small handful of toys and put them onto their counting mat. Now ask each child to count their toys and to say how many they have. Now say *If Jemima takes away two toys how many do you think she will have left?* Encourage the children to make the prediction, then ask the child that you named to remove two toys and say how many is left. Check to see how they do this, for example by counting one by one what is left on the mat. Repeat this with the other children.

As the children work ask probing questions such as:
● *If I took two of your toys how many would you have then?*
● *What happens when we take away in maths?*
● *Make up your own take away question and show how to do it.*

Plenary
Put out a set of eight counting toys and ask a child to count these. Now say *How many toys are there? So how many will there be if we take away two?* Ask for responses and how the children worked that out. Now invite a child to remove two toys and to say what is left as a check. Repeat this several times for quantities of toys up to ten.

Possible difficulties	Next steps
Children may still have difficulties with counting sets.	Provide further experience of counting sets of toys. Begin with small quantities up to five until the child is confident, then extend to up to ten. When they are confident with counting sets, return to work on taking away, initially working with a starting set of up to five or six toys.

Help sheet for Taking away

Ask the children to sit at a table, each with a work mat and counting toys in a pot in front of them. Explain that you will ask each child to take a small handful of toys and put them onto their counting mat. Now ask each child to count their toys and to say how many they have. Now say: *If Jemima takes away two toys how many do you think she will have left?* Encourage the children to make the prediction, then ask the child that you named to remove two toys and say how many is left. Check to see how they do this, for example by counting one by one what is left on the mat. Repeat this with the other children.

As the children work ask probing questions such as:

- *If I took two of your toys how many would you have then?*
- *What happens when we take away in maths?*
- *Make up your own take away question and show how to do it.*

Record the children's achievements. It would be helpful to record which children take away with confidence and which children had difficulties and what those difficulties were.

Child's name	Demonstrated confidence	Had difficulties

Counting objects record

Each entry should include the date and should give an indication of how far the child can count reliably.

Child's name	Can count by touching, moving and counting	Can count by touching and counting	Can count by pointing and counting	Can count sounds	Can count along a track

Assess and Review

Key objectives to be assessed
Assessment lesson 1: **Begin to relate addition to combining two groups of objects.**
Assessment lesson 2: **Talk about, recognise and recreate simple patterns.**

Photocopiable pages
'Help sheet for Combining' (see page 103), 'Help sheet for Making patterns' (see page 105), 'Counting objects record' (see page 100) 'Counting pictures' (see page 106)

Equipment
Red and blue counters; red, blue, yellow and purple beads; lace; 1-9 Number cards per group; two sorting hoops; ten counting toys; 20 containers in three different colours; three beanbags in each of four colours; large hoop.

Assessment Activities

Mental maths assessment

1. Counting to 20 [a]
Ask a group of children to count to 20, together. They can gently swing their arms or punch the air to keep a rhythm. Ask the children to repeat their count several times. Now ask them to count around the circle several times: *zero, one, two, three, …20.* Ensure that a different child says zero each time.

Probing questions
● *Why is it important that we say the numbers in the same order each time when we count?*

Practical maths assessment

1. Numbers 1 to 9 [c]
Work with a pair of children and with a shuffled set of 1-9 number cards. Ask the children to take turns to turn over a card and to say the number.

Probing questions
● *Tell me how you know this number says five.*
● *I am thinking of a number. It has a straight line across the top. What could it be?*

2. More and less [d]
Put out six counting toys in one sorting hoop and four in the other. Ask each group: *Which has more/less? How can you tell?* Repeat this for other quantities.

Probing questions
● *Which would you rather have: four sweets or seven sweets? Why?*
● *Which has more/less? How can you tell?*

3. Counting [b]
Give each child a copy of 'Counting pictures'. Ask them to look at the picture cards and invite each child to find the picture with a given number of fish. Observe how the children count. Do they touch, or point? Record the children's progress on the 'Counting objects record sheet'.

Probing questions
● *Find me the picture that has eight fish, five fish etc.*
● *How can you be sure that you have counted all the fish? Can you check in a different way?*

4. Position I-Spy [j]
Say some position statements about things in the home area, such as *I spy something on top of the cupboard; I spy something under the chair…* When the children have responded, encourage them to say where things are, eg, *I spy the telephone; I spy the teddy…*

Probing questions
● *Where is the ___? What can I see on top of… the ___?*

4. Beanbag throw [d]
Make a line with chalk, or with masking tape. Invite the children to take turns to throw a beanbag into the hoop. When they have all had two turns ask:

Probing questions
● *Which of your beanbags is nearer to/further away from the hoop? How can you tell?*
● *Which is the longer/shorter throw?*

Combining

Key objective
Begin to relate addition to combining two groups of objects.

What you need
● Copy of 'Help sheet for Combining'
● two copies of 'Work mat 2' (page 89)
● ten small counting toys.

Further support
● If children have difficulty with combining two groups, ask the children to count each of the two sets and say how many toys there are.
● Now, together, count again, from one of the sets, counting on to the second set. Repeat this and check that the children can count all by counting one set then counting on to the second set.
● When they are confident with that say *How many are there here? So we can count on from there for this set like this...* and model counting on from a given quantity.

Oral and mental starter
Ask the children to hold up the number of fingers that you say. Say for example: *Show me four fingers. Now show me seven fingers.* Repeat this several times for quantities of fingers between zero and ten. Now explain that you will hold up some fingers. Ask the children to put up their hands to say how many.

Main assessment activity
This is an assessment activity for pairs of children and an adult. Provide the adult with 'Help sheet for Combining' and, before the activity, remind the adult that you will need to know which children tackled the activity well and understood, and which children need further help and what they found difficult.

Work with two children. Ask one of the children to count out three toys to go onto one work mat, and then count out two toys to go onto the second work mat. Ask the other child to check the count each time. Now ask the first child *How many toys are there here? And here? So how many toys are there altogether? How will you find out?* Listen to, and watch, the strategies that the child uses. Check that they either count one set of toys, then the other, then count all, or count on from one set to the other.

As the children work, ask probing questions such as:
● *Which mat has more on it? How do you know?*
● *How many are there altogether? How did you work that out?*

Repeat this for other quantities, keeping the total to no more than ten.

Plenary
Repeat the starter activity, this time ask the children to show a quantity of fingers on one hand, from one to five, then another on the second hand, again from one to five. Now say: *How many fingers is that altogether?* Watch to see which children count all and which count on from one hand. This will give some indication of how confident children are with combining by counting on.

Possible difficulties	Next steps
Child counts both sets separately, but cannot combine the count.	Provide further experience in counting individual sets until the child is confident with that. Then ask them to count one set, and another. Now ask: *How many are there altogether?* Model counting one, then straight on to the next to count all: for three and two, count: one, two, three, four, five. Repeat this in different contexts until the child is confident.

Help sheet for Combining

You will need:

- Ten small counting toys
- two copies of 'Work mat 2' (page 89).

Work with two children. Ask one of the children to count out three toys to go onto one work mat, and then count out two toys to go onto the second work mat. Ask the other child to check the count each time. Now ask the first child: *How many toys are there here? And here? So how many toys are there altogether? How will you find out?* Listen to, and watch, the strategies that the child uses. Check that they either count one set of toys, then the other, then count all, or count on from one set to the other.

As the children work, ask probing questions such as:

- *Which mat has more on it? How do you know?*
- *How many are there altogether? How did you work that out?*

Repeat this for other quantities, keeping the total to no more than ten.

Record the children's achievements. It would be helpful to record how children total such as counting all, or counting on from one of the sets, and which children had difficulties and what those difficulties were.

Child's name	Demonstrated confidence	Had difficulties

Making patterns

What you need
- Red and blue counters
- red and blue beads
- yellow and purple beads
- lace
- activity sheet 'Help sheet for Making patterns'

Further support
- Where children find this activity difficult, ask them to make a pattern that you say, such as red, blue, red, blue...
- When they have put out the counters, ask the children to say the pattern with you, pointing to each counter as they say its colour.
- Now ask them to put down the next counter in the pattern, and the next, each time saying its name.

Oral and mental starter

Begin by threading a lace with beads: red, blue, red, blue... and ask *What comes next? And next?* Now thread another lace with a different pattern, such as red, blue, blue, red, blue, blue... and repeat.

Main assessment activity

This is an assessment activity for four children and an adult. Provide the adult with 'Help sheet for Making patterns' and, before the activity, remind the adult that you will need to know which children tackled the activity well and understood, and which children need further help and what they found difficult.

Using the counters the adult makes a row of red, blue, red, blue, then asks:
- *What pattern can you see?*
- *What comes next... and next...?*
- *How do you know?*

Now ask the children to shut their eyes. Remove one counter from the pattern and close it up. Say:
- *Look at my pattern. What is wrong with it?*
- *How can I put the pattern right?*

Now invite each child to make a pattern with some counters. Ask:
- *What pattern could you make with these counters?*
- *Can you make a different pattern?*
- *Say your pattern for me. What comes next... and next...?*

Plenary

Using the lace and beads, make a new pattern, this time with different colours, such as yellow and purple. Begin with, for example, yellow, yellow, purple, purple, yellow, yellow... and, pointing to each bead, ask the children to say the pattern with you. Now ask: *What will come next in my pattern? And next?* Now ask for suggestions from the children for a new pattern. Invite a child to make the pattern with the beads, and ask the other children to say what will come next and next, as before.

Possible difficulties	Next steps
Does not continue a pattern accurately.	Provide further experiences of copying patterns with real objects. For example, make a pattern with coloured cubes, and ask the child to copy it. When the child is confident with this, ask them to say what comes next... and next... in the pattern.

Help sheet for Making patterns

You will need about 20 red and 20 blue counters.

Using the counters make a row of red, blue, red, blue, then ask:
- What pattern can you see?
- What comes next... and next...?
- How do you know?

Now ask the children to shut their eyes. Remove one counter from the pattern and close it up. Ask:
- Look at my pattern. What is wrong with it?
- How can I put the pattern right?

Now invite each child to make a pattern with some counters. Ask:
- What pattern could you make with these counters?
- Can you make a different pattern?
- Say your pattern for me. What comes next? and next?

Record the children's achievements. It would be helpful to record which children can make and describe patterns with confidence and which children had difficulties and what those difficulties were.

Child's name	Demonstrated confidence	Had difficulties

Counting pictures

ALL NEW 100 MATHS HOMEWORK AND ASSESSMENT · YEAR R

www.scholastic.co.uk

Observation grid

The probing questions below can be used while the children are engaged in everyday mathematical activities.

Decide whether to use these assessment questions during a relevant unit of work, or at the end of term during the 'Assess and review' activities. A section has been included to add comments for individual children.

Child's name _____ **Date** _____

Green Stepping Stones	Probing questions	Comments
Show confidence with numbers by initiating or requesting number activities.	How many are there? How do you know that?	
Count out up to six objects from a larger group.	Count out 3/4/5/6 for me. When you counted, what was the last number you said? How many are there?	
Count actions or objects that cannot be moved.	Count the pictures. When you counted what was the last number you said? How many are there?	
Count an irregular arrangement of up to 10 objects.	*(Show the children an irregular arrangement of objects.)* How are you going to count these? How do you know that you have counted all of them?	
Begin to count beyond 10.	Count to 10/beyond 10. How far do you think you can count? Show me.	
Recognise numerals 1 to 5, then 1 to 9.	What number is this? Tell me a number with a straight line. What numbers have a curved line?	

WEEK 12 🔲 **End of term assessment**

Observation grid

Child's name _____ Date _____

Green Stepping Stones	Probing questions	Comments
Begin to use mathematical names for 'solid' 3D shapes and 'flat' 2D shapes and mathematical terms to describe shapes. Choose suitable components to make a particular model.	What is the same/different about these two shapes? What is this shape called? Which shapes did you choose to make this? Why are these good for building a ___? What other shapes could you have chosen?	
Order two items by capacity. Order two or three items by length.	Which do you think holds more/less? Do you think all of this water will fit in here? Which do you think is longer/wider/narrower/shorter? How can you check?	
Count up to three or four objects by saying one number name for each item.	(*Listening to the puppet count: 1, 2, 3, 3, 4; 1, 2, 3, 5, 6.*) What did the puppet do wrong? What should he say?	
Sometimes show confidence and offer solutions to problems.	How many do you think we can have each? How can we find out?	
Show awareness of symmetry. Find items from positional/directional clues. Describe a simple journey. Instruct a programmable toy.	(*Make a paper chain.*) What shapes will this be when we open it out? (*Playing positional 'I-Spy'.*) Where is the ___? Point to the ___. Tell me how to get from ___ to ___. What instructions did you give to the Roamer? How do you need to change the Roamer's instructions?	
Find the total number of items in two groups by counting all of them.	(*Children to take two handfuls of cubes and say how many in each hand.*) How many altogether? How did you find out?	

PHOTOCOPIABLE

Assess and Review

Key objectives to be assessed
Assessment lesson 1: **Recognise numerals 1 to 9.**
Assessment lesson 2: **Use language such as more or less, greater or smaller, heavier or lighter, to compare two numbers or quantities.**

Photocopiable pages
Copy of 'Help sheet for recognising numerals' for adult Helpers (page 111), 'Numeral cards 0-9' (page 114); 'Help sheet for measures' for adult Helpers (page 113).

Equipment
Large teaching numeral cards 1-9; bucket balance with items for comparing (eg bricks, small toys, cubes), pairs of items to compare for length (eg teddies, ribbons), basket containing scarves of different lengths; 20 counters in three different colours; plate with nine pieces of play food on it.

Assessment Activities

Mental maths assessment
Counting a
With a group, count to 20 from zero and back. Encourage them to keep the pace by swinging their arms or punching the air in time as they count. When the children have repeated the count several times, and it is clearly a confident count, invite the children to count around the circle from zero to 20 and back again: zero, one, two, three... 20, 19, 18... Repeat this several times, and ensure that a different child says zero each time.
Probing questions
● *Why do we have to say the number names in the same order each time?*

Practical maths assessment
1. Patterns h
Ask groups to use three colours of counters to make patterns, such as ABCABC... Ask the children to say the pattern and to say what comes next. Now ask them to shut their eyes. Alter the pattern either by removing a counter, or by adding a counter. Ask the children to open their eyes and identify any changes.
Probing questions
● *What comes next? and next?*
● *Is my pattern right? What is wrong with this pattern? How can it be put right?*

2. Problems k
Working with a group of four children, put a plate of play food onto the table and ask: *How many times do you think I can pass the plate around the table? Why do you think that?* Now ask the children to pass the plate and each take a piece of play food. Ask: *How much is left on the plate? Can we pass the plate again? Will you all have a piece?* Pass the plate, so that the children can check their answer. Ask about what is left. Say: *I'll give this one to Sadie. That's fair isn't it?* Check that the children understand that this is or is not fair and can explain why.
Probing questions
● *How many times can we pass the plate?*
● *Is this fair? Why do you think that?*

Recognising numerals

Key objective
Recognise numerals 1 to 9.

What you need
1 to 9 numeral cards from 'Numeral cards 0–9' (page 114)
● copies of 'Help sheet for Recognising numerals' (page 111) for adult Helpers
● large teaching numeral cards for 1 to 9.

Further support
● Where children do not yet recognise all of the numerals from one to nine, begin with the numeral cards for one to five and use the above activity for these numerals.
● Over time, this can be repeated, extending the range of numerals to check which numerals children recognise.

Oral and mental starter

Ask the children to sit in a circle. Begin by saying the counting numbers from one to nine forwards, then back again to one. Now ask the children to count around the circle, each child saying the next number. If a child falters, say the number to maintain the pace.

Main assessment activity

This activity is suitable for groups of three children working with an adult. Provide the adult with a copy of 'Help sheet for Recognising numerals'.

Shuffle a set of 1–9 numeral cards and give each child a card, at random. Ask them to show the other children their cards and to read the number. Repeat this until all the cards have been given out. Now ask the children to take turns to find the cards in counting order, starting with one, and to place the cards out in a line. Say, for example: *Which card do we need first? Yes, one. Now which card do we need to put down? Who has that?*

Shuffle the cards again, and repeat the activity, so that each child has the opportunity over time to read several numerals.

Ask probing questions as the children work, such as:
● *Tell me how you know this number is a three and this is a five.*
● *I'm thinking of a number with a straight line across the top. Which number could it be? Which numbers could it not be? Why not?*

Plenary

Ask the children to sit in front of you. Show them the large numeral cards and shuffle these. Now show the children each card in turn and ask: *Which number is this?* Give the numeral card to the child who answers correctly. When all the cards have been handed out, ask the children with the cards to stand at the front, in any order, holding out their card for the others to see. Now invite the children to help to order the children into number order. When this is done, say, for example: *Yasmin, change places with the person who is holding the number...* This will give further opportunities for assessing children's abilities to recognise the numerals 1 to 9.

Possible difficulty	Next step
Does not differentiate between numerals with similar appearance, such as three and five; six and nine, etc.	Provide further experience of recognising numerals, including opportunities to trace around textured numeral templates. Discuss the features of the numerals and compare those that are confusing so that the child begins to recognise the differences.

Help sheet for Recognising numerals

You will need
– 'Numeral cards 0–9' (page 114).

Work with a group of three children at a table. Shuffle 1–9 numeral cards from the set and give each child a card, at random. Ask them to show the other children their cards and to read the number. Repeat this until all the cards have been given out. Now ask the children to take turns to find the cards in counting order, starting with one, and to place the cards out in a line. Say, for example: *Which card do we need first? Yes, one. Now which card do we need to put down? Who has that?*

Shuffle the cards again, and repeat the activity, so that each child has the opportunity over time to read several numerals.

Ask probing questions as the children work, such as:
◾ *Tell me how you know this number is a three and this a five.*
◾ *I'm thinking of a number with a straight line across the top. Which number could it be? Which numbers could it not be? Why not?*

Record the children's achievements. It would be helpful to record which children recognise the numerals with ease and which children had difficulties and what those difficulties were, including any confusions between two numerals.

Child's name	Demonstrated confidence	Had difficulties

Measures

<table>
<tr><td>

Key objective
Use language such as more or less, longer or shorter, heavier or lighter... to compare two quantities.

What you need
● Bucket balance and items for comparing such as bricks, small toys or cubes
● pairs of items to compare for length such as teddies, ribbons, strips of paper, pencils
● copy of 'Help sheet for Measures' (page 113) for adult Helpers
● basket containing scarves of various lengths.

Further support
● Where children are not yet confident with comparing lengths make the comparisons by placing one end of each teddy level so that the children can compare the other end.
● For balancing, discuss how to tell if two items balance by looking at the bucket balance.

</td><td>

Oral and mental starter
Show the children the basket of scarves. Invite two children to each choose a scarf. Now invite the children to compare the scarves. Ask questions such as:
● *Which scarf is longer/shorter?*
● *Which scarf is wider/narrower?*
● *How can you tell?*

Main assessment activity
Set up the activities which can be found on 'Help sheet for Measures'. Provide adult helpers with the Help sheet and discuss which activity you would like each adult to support.

For the Balancing activity, check that children understand what represents 'balance', that is that they recognise that when the two pans are horizontal that the items balance. Ask questions as the children work, such as:
● *Which do you think is heavier/lighter?*
● *Did you make a good guess?*
● *Look at the balance.* (With an item on each side, and not in balance). *Which is heavier/lighter? How can you tell?*

For the Comparing length activity, check that children make a direct comparison and that they understand that by putting one end of each item level they can then compare the other end of each for length. Questions can include:
● *Which is longer/shorter? How do you know? Show me.*
● *Which is narrower/wider? Show me how you know that.*
● *Which is thicker/thinner? Show me how you know that.*

Plenary
Place a small toy in one bucket of the balance. Invite a child to balance it by adding bricks or cubes to the other bucket until balance is achieved. Ask:
● *How can you tell that these bricks balance the toy?*
● *What would happen if I added some more bricks to this bucket... that bucket?*

</td></tr>
</table>

Possible difficulty	Next step
Child does not match two ends of an item for comparing lengths and instead looks at which item 'sticks out' further.	Give more experience of comparing lengths by matching one end and considering the other for which is longer/shorter.
Child does not recognise how to tell which is heavier, lighter or about the same from the position of the buckets on a balance.	Provide further experience of using a bucket balance. Encourage the child to make the buckets balance, then add more to one of the buckets. Ask: *Which is heavier/lighter? How can you tell?*

Help sheet for Measures

Balancing

You will need some items for weighing, and a bucket balance. Work with pairs of children. Ask the children to each choose two items and estimate which is heavier, and which is lighter, by holding them in their hands. Ask the children to check by using the balance.

Ask probing questions such as:

◀ Which do you think is heavier... lighter?

◀ Did you make a good guess?

◀ Look at the balance. (With an item on each side, and not in balance). Which is heavier/lighter? How can you tell?

Comparing length

You will need items for comparing length, such as toys, paintbrushes, scissors and so on.

Put the items for comparing length on the table. Work with a group of about four children. Ask them to choose two items each. Ask each child:

◀ Which is longer/shorter? How do you know? Show me.

◀ Which is narrower/wider? Show me how you know that.

◀ Which is thicker/thinner? Show me how you know that.

SUMMER ASSESSMENT

Numeral cards 0–9

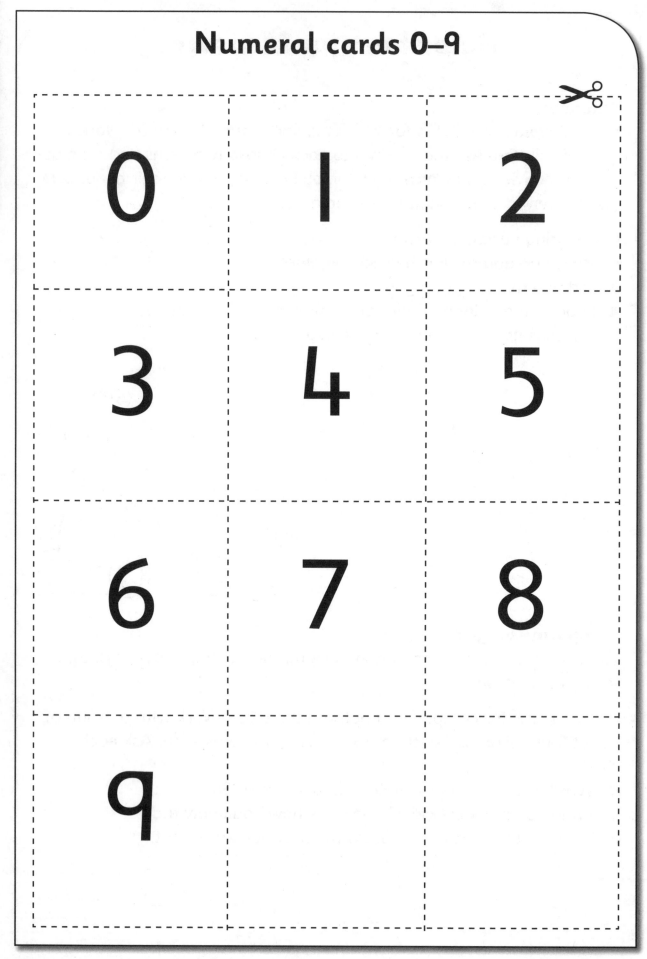

Assess and Review

Key objectives to be assessed
Assessment lesson 1: **Use developing mathematical ideas and methods to solve practical problems.**
Assessment lesson 2: **Use everyday words to describe position.**

Photocopiable pages
'Help sheet for solving problems' (page 117) and 'Help sheet for Position' (page 119) for adult helpers; 'Coin cards' (page 120).

Equipment
Class shop with items priced from 1p to 10p; PE equipment such as hoops, and beanbags; doll's house, dolls and furniture; mixed coins

Assessment Activities

Practical maths assessment
1. Doll's house [j]
Work with a pair of children. Ask them to follow your instructions for putting furniture and the dolls into the doll's house. Say, for example: *Put the bed next to the wardrobe. Put the cup on top of the table...* Continue in this way, so that the children hear and can respond to a range of positional language. When the items are back in the dolls house invite the children to respond to questions of the *Where is the___?* variety.
Probing question
● *Tell me where the ___ is?*
● *Put ___ on the bed/behind the bed/under the bed/in front of the bed.*

2. Problems [k]
Work with two children to solve some money problems. Ask one of the children to be the shopkeeper and the other the customer. Say: *The customer buys a lolly for 4p. How much change will the shopkeeper give? How did you work that out?* Observe the strategies that the children use. For example, they might exchange the 5p coin for four 1p coins; alternately, they might count on from 4p to find the 1p. Repeat this for other similar problems keeping the amounts of money involved less than 10p.
Probing question
● *Do you have enough money? How do you know that?*
● *How did you work it out?*
● *Is there another way?*

Solving problems

Key objective
Use developing mathematical ideas and methods to solve practical problems.

What you need
● A class shop with items priced from 1p to 10p; 1p, 2p, 5p and 10p coins
● copy of 'Help sheet for Solving problems' (page 117)
● 1p, 2p, 5p, 10p, 20p, 50p, £1 and £2 teaching coin cards.

Further support
● Where children are not yet confident with subtraction from ten, limit the range of prices to up to 5p, and ask the customer to give a 5p coin each time.
● You may prefer to use just 1p coins for giving change.

Oral and mental starter
Explain that you will show the children some coin cards. Ask them to put up their hands to say which coin is on the picture. Begin with low value coins 1p, 2p and 5p, then move to the higher values. Ask questions such as:
● *How many pennies are worth the same as a 2p/5p/10p coin?*
● *What colour is a ___ coin?*

Main assessment activity
This is an activity for a group of about four children. If an adult Helper is to work with a group provide a copy of 'Help sheet for Solving problems'. Work either in the class shop, or move some of the priced items to a table, with the coins.

Ask the children to take turns to be customer and shopkeeper. The customer chooses an item to buy and shows the shopkeeper its price. He or she then gives the shopkeeper a 10p coin. The shopkeeper works out the change from 10p. Repeat this several times so that each child has several turns at being both customer and shopkeeper.

Watch how the shopkeeper gives the change. At this stage, expect the children to count out the change in 1p coins. However, do note any child who is able to use coins worth 2p or 5p as part of the change-giving process .

As the children work ask probing questions such as:
● *How did you work that out?*
● *How did you know that it was a counting back problem?*

Plenary
Have a pot of small denomination coins available. Choose something from the shop which costs 5p. Show the item and ask: *How much does this cost? What coins could I use to pay for this exactly?* Invite children to come to the front and choose some coins to pay, so that each time the coin range is different. Record each one on the flipchart like this: 1p 1p 1p 1p 1p; 2p 2p 1p; and so on so that the children can check if they have found the same way, but with the coins in a different order, or a new way to pay. Repeat this for different prices. This is an opportunity to see which children can total small numbers. Invite children to explain how they totalled.

Possible difficulty	Next step
Child counts any coin as 'one'.	Provide further experience of putting out equivalent values for 2p and 5p coins using pennies. Extend this to the 10p coin over time.

Help sheet for Solving problems

You will need a pot of 1p, 2p, 5p and 10p coins and some items from the class shop priced from 1p to 10p.

Work with a group of about four children.

Ask the children to take turns to be customer and shopkeeper. The customer chooses an item to buy and shows the shopkeeper its price. The customer gives the shopkeeper a 10p coin. The shopkeeper works out the change from 10p. Repeat this several times so that each child has several turns at being both customer and shopkeeper.

Watch how the shopkeeper gives the change. At this stage, expect the children to count out the change in 1p coins. However, do note any child who is able to use higher-value coins as part of giving change.

As the children work ask probing questions such as:
- How did you work that out?
- How did you know that it was a counting back problem?

Record the children's achievements. It would be helpful to record the method that children used to give change, which children were not yet confident and what difficulties they had, such as counting each coin as worth 'one'.

Child's name	Demonstrated confidence	Had difficulties

Position

> ### Key objective
> Use everyday words to describe position.

> ### What you need
> ● PE equipment such as hoops, benches, beanbag
> ● 'Help sheet for Position' (page 119).

> ### Further support
> ● Provide a copy of 'Help sheet for Position' (page 119) for an adult
> ● Ask them to take a small group of children who are not sure about the vocabulary, and demonstrate what each word means, then put it into a sentence for the children to follow.

Oral and mental starter

Play I spy. Say, for example, *I can see something on top of the cupboard... on the bookcase... under the table...* Ask the children to put up their hands to suggest what the item is. Children who are really confident with this can give I spy clues for their classmates to solve.

Main assessment activity

This activity can be undertaken with all the children. Concentrate on a group of children, in turn. You may want to repeat the activity over time, until all children have been assessed for their ability to understand and follow position instructions.

Ask the children to get changed for a PE session, or an activity session outside.

Use position words, such as: *position, over, under, above, below, top, bottom, side, on, in, outside, inside, around, in front of, behind, front, back, before, after, beside, next to, opposite, apart, between* to give instructions. For example, say: *Stand beside a partner. Now stand opposite your partner. Stand with your backs to each other. Stand inside/outside a hoop... Stand on/behind/in front of the bench.*

Check that the children that you are targeting for this activity do follow the instructions, without watching to see what others do in order to get clues.

As the children work, ask probing questions of individuals such as:
● *Where are you standing?*
● *Who/what is next to you?*

Plenary

Play I-Spy again, as in the starter, back in the classroom. Encourage children to take turns to say *I spy something...* then to use a positional word to describe where the object is. Encourage some of the children who are less confident to demonstrate what they can do, even if they wish to whisper their 'I spy...' to you to say to the rest of the class. This will give further opportunities to identify those who are confident in using position vocabulary and those who need further experience.

Possible difficulty	Next step
Does not follow instructions which include position vocabulary.	Provide further experience of following instructions. For example, ask an adult to work with a small group with small-world toys such as a doll's house, garage, farm... Ask the adult to say where to put some of the toys. Then they swap roles and the child can instruct the adult. Here it is helpful if the adult makes mistakes for the child to correct!

Help sheet for Position

Work in the hall with a group of children.

The teacher will use position words, such as: *position, over, under, above, below, top, bottom, side, on, in, outside, inside, around, in front of, behind, front, back, before, after, beside, next to, opposite, apart, between to give instructions.* For example, say: *Stand beside a partner. Now stand opposite your partner. Stand with your backs to each other. Stand inside/ outside a hoop... Stand on/behind/in front of... the bench.*

Check that the children that you are working with for this activity do follow the instructions, without watching to see what others do in order to get clues.

As the children work, ask probing questions of individuals such as:
◼ *Where are you standing?*
◼ *Who/what is next to you?*

If children are unsure, provide further help by modelling the instructions yourself, then asking the children to copy you.

Record the children's achievements. It would be helpful to record which children follow the position instructions with ease and which children had difficulties and what those difficulties were, including any vocabulary that they did not understand.

Child's name	Demonstrated confidence	Had difficulties

Coin cards

PHOTOCOPIABLE

www.scholastic.co.uk

Observation grid

The probing questions below can be used while the children are engaged in everyday mathematical activities.

Decide whether to use these assessment questions during a relevant unit of work, or at the end of term during the 'Assess and review' activities. A section has been included to add comments for individual children.

Child's name _____ **Date** _____

Green Stepping Stones	Probing questions	Comments
Show confidence with numbers by initiating or requesting number activities.	How many are there? How do you know that?	
Count out up to six objects from a larger group.	Count out 3... 4...5... 6. What was the last number you said?	
Count an irregular arrangement of up to 10 objects.	(*Show an irregular arrangement of objects.*) How are you going to count these? How do you know that you have counted all of them?	
Show increased confidence with numbers by spotting errors.	(*Use a puppet to put out the number cards 1 to 9: 1, 2, 3, 5, 6, 4, 7, 8, 9.*) Is this correct? What has the puppet done wrong? Can you put it right?	
Recognise some numerals of personal significance.	How old are you? Can you find the number card for ___?	
Recognise numerals 1 to 5, then 1 to 9.	What number is this? Tell me a number with a straight line/curved line.	
Select the correct numeral to represent 1 to 5, then 1 to 9, objects.	How many ___ are there? Which number card do you need for that amount?	
Begin to represent numbers using fingers, marks on paper or pictures.	How many are there? Can you make that many dots on paper? Use your arm in the air to show	

PHOTOCOPIABLE

WEEK 12 🔲 **End of term assessment**

Observation grid

Child's name _____ Date _____

Green Stepping Stones	Probing questions	Comments
Order two items by weight.	Which do you think is heavier/ lighter? How can you check?	
Sometimes show confidence and offer solutions to problems.	How many do you think we can have each? How can we find out?	
Show awareness of symmetry.	(*Make a paper chain.*) What shape will this be when we open it?	
Find items from positional/ directional clues.	(*Playing positional I-Spy.*) Where is the ___? Point to the ___.	
Describe a simple journey.	Tell me how to get from ___ to ___.	
Instruct a programmable toy.	What instructions did you give the Roamer?	
Choose suitable components to make a particular model.	How do you need to change the Roamer's instructions?	
Select a particular named shape.	What is the same/different about these two shapes? What is this shape called? Which shapes did you choose to make this? Why are these good for building a ___? What other shapes could you have chosen?	

End-of-year assessments

On pages 124–127, you will find two alternative plans for assessing children's achievements over the year. The assessments are built from play contexts and include:
- In the café
- The sand tray

For each assessment, notes on setting up the play area and administering the assessment are given along with two prompt sheets (on pages 125 and 127). Each prompt sheet contains a set of probing questions matched to each of the NNS key objectives for Reception. All of the probing questions are set in the context and either assessment will offer rich opportunities to assess the children's understanding and use of mathematical language across the range of objectives.

SUMMER ASSESSMENT

In the café

Preparation

Create a café in your setting. This can have: a till with some coins; paper and crayons for taking orders; ten of each item of play food such as cakes, biscuits and jellies (in a variety of shapes and sizes including cubes, pyramids, cones and spheres); paper plates; various-sized beakers; jugs, water coloured with food dye; shape tiles for squares, rectangles, triangles, circles and stars; a bucket balance; feely box or bag; 'Numeral cards 0–9' (photocopiable page 114).

What to do

Work with pairs of children.

◼ Put some cakes and biscuits on separate plates. Invite the children to choose a plate of cakes or biscuits and to count how many there are.

◼ Ask the children to find the number card to show how many cakes they have counted.

◼ Give the children different food items to weigh or measure.

◼ Provide play food or packaging of different shapes and sizes for the children to identify shapes.

In the café prompt sheet

Key objectives	Probing questions
a) Say and use number names in order in familiar contexts.	Why do we have to say the numbers in the same order each time when we count?
b) Count reliably up to 10 everyday objects.	What was the last number you said? So how many cakes/biscuits are on the plate?
c) Recognise numerals 1 to 9.	Which number card shows that number? What other numbers have a straight line at the top/curves?
d) Use language such as more or less, greater or smaller, heavier or lighter, to compare two numbers or quantities.	Each of you take some of the cakes. How many have you each? Who has more/fewer? How can you tell? Each of you choose two jellies. Which one do you think is heavier/lighter? Why? How can you check? Did you make a good guess? Each of you choose two beakers. Which one do you think will hold more/less? Why? How can you check? Each of you take some of the money from the till. Make a line of coins. Who do you think has made the longer/shorter line? Why? How can you check?
e) In practical activities and discussion, begin to use the vocabulary involved in adding and subtracting.	Here are five cakes for you and two cakes for me. How can we find out how many there are altogether? Show me. Here are five cakes. If you take away three cakes how many would there be? How can you find out? Show me.
f) Find one more or one less than a number from 1 to 10.	Here are three biscuits. If I give you one more/take one away, how many would you have? How did you work it out?
g) Begin to relate addition to combining two groups of objects, and subtraction to 'taking away'.	Here are four biscuits and here are three more. How many are there altogether? How did you work that out? Here are eight biscuits. If I take three away how many would you have then? How did you work that out?
h) Talk about, recognise and recreate simple patterns.	Look at the pattern I have made (for example, biscuit, cake, cake, biscuit, cake, cake...). What comes next? And next? Can you make a different pattern with the biscuits and cakes?
i) Use language such as circle or bigger to describe the shape and size of solids and flat shapes.	Put some of the cake shapes into the feely box. Can you find me a cake that is shaped like a cube? How do you know that you have found a cube? Repeat this with the 2D shape tiles.
j) Use everyday words to describe position.	(Put a cake on top of the till/underneath some paper/inside the jug... .) Where is the cake?
k) Use developing mathematical ideas and methods to solve practical problems.	Can you put five cakes on each plate? Can you put the same number of biscuits on each plate? Are there enough biscuits? Why do you think that? Share out the biscuits. Were you right? Is this fair?

The sand tray

Equipment

Sand tray with dry sand; sand equipment such as buckets, spades and moulds; nine shells; a bucket balance; cubes, spheres, pyramids, cones; shape tiles for squares, rectangles, triangles, circles and stars; 0–9 numeral cards (photocopiable page 116).

What to do

◼ Bury ten shells in the sand. Say: *How many shells can you find?*

◼ Invite the children to find the number card to show how many shells they have found.

◼ Provide buckets, spades and so on for the children to compare and weigh.

◼ Put 2D and 3D shapes in the sand for the children to identify.

The sand tray prompt sheet

Key objectives	Probing questions
a) Say and use the number names in order in familiar contexts.	Why do we have to say the numbers in the same order each time when we count?
b) Count reliably up to 10 everyday objects.	What was the last number you said? So how many shells have you found?
c) Recognise numerals 1 to 9.	Bury some plastic numbers in the sand. Which number card shows that number? Which numbers have a straight line/curves at the top?
d) Use language such as more or less, greater or smaller, heavier or lighter, to compare two numbers or quantities.	Each of you take some shells. How many do each of you have? Who has more/fewer? How can you tell? Each of you choose two moulds/ buckets/spades. Tell me which is the heaviest/ longest/holds more. Why? How can you check? Did you make a good estimate?
e) In practical activities and discussion, begin to use the vocabulary involved in adding and subtracting.	Here are four shells for you and three shells for me. How can we find out how many there are altogether? Show me. Here are six shells. If you take away three shells how many would there be? How can you find out? Tell me.
f) Find one more or one less than a number from 1 to 10.	Here are four shells. If I give you one more/take one away, how many would you have? How did you work it out?
g) Begin to relate addition to combining two groups of objects, and subtraction to 'taking away'.	Here are three shells and here are two more. How many altogether? How did you work that out? Here are seven shells. If I take two away how many would you have? How did you work that out?
h) Talk about, recognise and recreate simple patterns.	Look at the pattern I have made (for example, shell, mould, shell, mould...). What comes next? Can you make a different pattern?
i) Use language such as circle or bigger to describe the shape and size of solids and flat shapes.	(Remove the sand toys. Bury some 3D shapes in the sand.) Feel in the sand. Can you find me a cube? How do you know that you have found a cube? (This can be repeated with 2D shape tiles.)
j) Use everyday words to describe position.	Put a cube on top of the bucket/underneath the bucket/inside the mould. Where is the bucket? (Ask 'where is' questions to check that the children can use positional language in response.)
k) Use developing mathematical ideas and methods to solve practical problems.	Can you make me three sand pies? Now here are the shells. How many shells are there? How many do you think we can put on each sand pie? Why? Share out the shells. Were you right? Is this fair?